Discovering History

Medieval Realms

ROS ADAMS

Series Editors
**NEIL TONGE &
PETER HEPPLEWHITE**

CPL

Causeway Press Ltd

To Rod and John

Acknowledgement

My thanks to the staff of Sandringham School for their help and support and also Ian Fisher, Mike Haralambos and Will Wale.

Ros Adams
September, 1991

Note to teachers

1. **The Focus pages**
   Each chapter contains a Focus page which aims to engage the reader, excite curiosity and raise issues. All Focus pages are based on primary source material from the Middle Ages.

2. **The Sources**
   Many of the written sources are translated paraphrases from the originals. The language has been adapted to aid comprehension.

   All original artwork is based on primary source material - either literary or archaeological.

3. **The Teachers' Guide**
   A teachers' guide is available. It is photocopiable and provides assessment tests, guidance for marking, advice for teaching, additional information and worksheets with further activities including games and simulations.

CONTENTS

1 INTRODUCTION

Imagine that England was invaded by a foreign army. That thousands died from war and thousands more from starvation and disease. That nearly every English person in an important position was replaced by a foreign invader. That English buildings were pulled to the ground and rebuilt in a foreign style. That the monarch was killed and replaced by a foreign king.

This is what happened when the Normans invaded England in 1066. England was not changed overnight but the changes were fast and often violent. To understand what happened we must look briefly at England before 1066.

Source A

Roman rule in Britain ended in 410. From the 5th century England was invaded by Angles and Saxons from what is now modern Germany. These tribes eventually created the kingdom of Anglo-Saxon England.

Source B   Places with Viking names

From the 9th century onwards Vikings from Denmark, Norway and Sweden invaded and settled in England. This map shows places which have Viking names. Anglo-Saxon kings fought many wars against the Vikings. England was ruled by Viking kings from 1016 to 1042.

Source C

Edward the Confessor being crowned King of England. He reigned from 1042-1066 and was succeeded by Harold, the last Anglo-Saxon king.

Anglo-Saxon England

Reading some of the things the Norman invaders wrote, you'd think that England in 1066 was a backward country. It wasn't. It was the richest country in western Europe. Its mints produced millions of silver coins. Its farmers were amongst the best in Europe. Its craftsmen built fine buildings and created beautiful works of art. Its monks wrote books on English history. Its government was well organised and efficient.

England was not a backwater on the outskirts of Europe. It was a rich prize for a foreign invader.

Source D   Anglo-Saxon craftsmanship

The Alfred Jewel, made of enamelled gold and crystal. It has an inscription round the edge which reads, 'Alfred had me made'.

Source E

Shepherds looking after sheep – a picture from an 11th century calendar. Wool was one of the main sources of England's wealth.

Source F   A chronicler

A page from Bede's *Ecclesiastical History* with an inset of the author at his writing desk. Much of the early history of England was written by monks such as Bede. These 'chroniclers' wrote about anything that interested them – not just religion, but politics, gossip and even the weather.

Activities

1. Draw a sketch map of Source A. Mark on where a) the Angles and Saxons, b) the Vikings and c) the Normans came from.

2. Look at Source B. Why do you think the Vikings settled in this part of England?

3. What evidence from this page suggests that England was a rich country?

4. Do you agree with the Normans that England was a backward country? Explain your answer.

5. Many of the sources used in this book were written by chroniclers. Like modern journalists and writers they had their own points of view. Their accounts are often one-sided or biased. Why is it important for you to know this for your study of medieval history?

2 THE NORMAN INVASION

The Norman army lands at Pevensey on the south coast of England.

The English army on Senlac Hill fight off the Norman cavalry.

The Norman cavalry attacks the English housecarls.

The pictures in this chapter are taken from the Bayeux Tapestry, an embroidery in coloured wools, 70 metres long and half a metre wide. It was made shortly after the Norman conquest and tells the story of William's invasion from the Norman point of view.

Themes

On January 5th 1066 King Edward the Confessor died. He had no children. Who was to be the next King of England?

Three men claimed the throne – Harold Godwine, a powerful English earl, Harold Hardrada, King of Norway and William, Duke of Normandy. On January 6th 1066 Harold Godwine was crowned king. England was a rich prize – the others would not take this lying down.

Harold Hardrada sailed from Norway with an army to take the crown by force. Harold Godwine defeated and killed him at Stamford Bridge near York on September 25th. Three days later William, Duke of Normandy, landed with an army on the south coast of England. He too was determined to take the crown by force. Harold Godwine marched 250 miles from the north and met the Norman army at Senlac Hill near Hastings.

This chapter asks the following questions.

- Why was Harold crowned King of England?
- Why did William think he should be king?

We start at the Battle of Hastings. The Focus describes the battle as a Norman soldier might have seen it. The description is based on sources written by the Normans.

Focus Activities

Read the passage opposite.

1. Why did the Normans win the Battle of Hastings? Give as many reasons as you can.

2. Write a description of the battle as it might have been seen by an English soldier.

The Battle of Hastings

By early morning of the 14th October 1066 we were standing at the bottom of Senlac Hill, just outside Hastings, looking up at the Saxon army. There, behind a hastily built wooden fence, stood the so-called King of England, Harold Godwine. Around him were the men of the fyrd – the Saxon army – some well-trained soldiers, but mostly local people, armed with clubs, axes and anything that would do as a weapon. The real professionals were Harold's bodyguard – the housecarls. Full-time warriors, they carried fearsome double-headed axes and used them to good effect. They were a terrifying sight.

Our leader, William, Duke of Normandy, drew up our troops. The armies were about the same size but as well as footsoldiers, armed with spears, shields and axes, and archers like myself, we also had cavalry – knights on horseback – which the English did not.

We attacked as soon as we could. We had to defeat the Saxons before their reinforcements arrived. Our orders were to break through the ring of housecarls and kill Harold. As long as he was alive Duke William could not count himself as king.

Our first attacks had little effect. My arrows just seemed to bounce off the Saxons' shield wall and the housecarls stood firm against the cavalry. A cry went round that William had been killed – not surprising really as I heard that he had three horses cut from under him during the battle. There was panic until the Duke removed his helmet to show that he was, indeed, still alive. A cheer went up and we fought all the harder.

Then came the move which won the battle. We pretended to retreat. Harold's men followed us. At the bottom of the hill we turned to fight. Here on the flat ground our cavalry gave us the advantage.

Then William ordered us to fire our arrows up into the air so that they rained down on the enemy's heads. Our troops pressed forward and attacked the housecarls under their shields. Harold was killed. I saw him and his bodyguard cut down by cavalrymen and hacked to pieces by our footsoldiers.

As dusk fell, the remaining Saxons fled into the woods. Our noble duke, William of Normandy, had won the crown of England by right of battle.

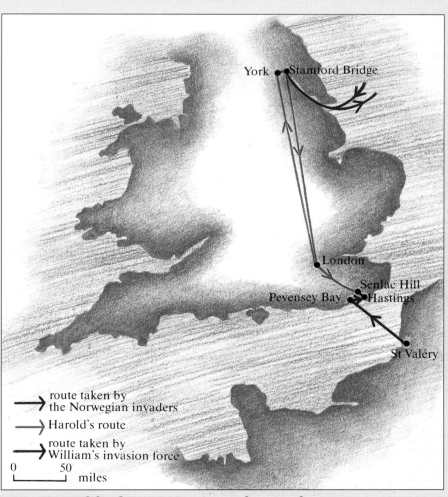

Movements of the three armies, September-October 1066

Harold Godwine

The sources on this page look at Harold's claim to the English throne. They were written by Saxons.

Harold was the most powerful nobleman in England. He was Earl of Wessex, which covered most of southern England. He had made a name for himself as a war leader by defeating the King of Gwynedd, the most powerful man in Wales.

During the last years of his reign, Edward the Confessor spent most of his time hunting, praying or organising the building of Westminster Abbey. Harold practically ruled the country for him.

Kings were usually chosen by the Witan – a meeting of earls and bishops, the most important men in England. On Edward's death the Witan chose Harold Godwine as the next King of England.

Activities

1. Why was it important for Harold that the Witan should choose him as king?

2. a) Look at Sources B, C and D. Copy and complete the table below.

	Possible reasons why Harold was chosen as king
Source B	
Source C	
Source D	

   b) Which do you think was the most likely reason? Explain your answer.

Source A

King Harold

Harold, son of Earl Godwine, was chosen king by the leading noblemen of all England (the Witan). On the same day Harold was crowned with great ceremony by Aldred, Archbishop of York.

'Chronicon ex Chronicis', c.1090

Source B

```
                              Earl Godwine
                         ┌──────────┴──────────┐
  Edward the                                    Harold
  Confessor    =   Edith                        Godwine
```

Harold and Edith were Earl Godwine's children. Edith was married to King Edward.

Source C

Harold Godwine and his brothers were earls and the king's favourites.

'Anglo-Saxon Chronicle', c.1053

Source D

Angels led the soul of King Edward to heaven. On his deathbed that wise king had promised the kingdom to Harold, a great noble. This was because Harold had always been loyal in word and deed: he had carried out all the king's commands and done what was needed.

'Anglo-Saxon Chronicle', c.1066

William of Normandy

The sources on this page look at William's claim to the English throne. All the sources are Norman.

William was Duke of Normandy in northern France. He was related to Edward the Confessor – his great aunt was Edward's mother. He claimed that during a visit to England in 1051 Edward had promised him that he would be the next king of England. He also claimed that Edward sent Harold Godwine to Normandy in 1064 to swear an oath (promise faithfully) that William should be the next king.

Source A

Edward, King of the English, loved William like a brother or son. The king was old, so he decided to make certain that William would be the next English king, as he had previously promised. He therefore sent Harold to William. This was so that Harold could swear an oath that William would be the next king. The reason Harold was chosen was this: he was a very great English noble and he would be able to support William if there was any trouble when King Edward died.

William of Poitiers, c.1070

Source C

The land of England was without her King Edward, and his crown was worn by Harold. This mad Englishman did not wait to be chosen, but, breaking his promise, seized the royal throne with the help of a few wicked followers.

William of Poitiers, c.1070

Source B

This picture comes from the Bayeux Tapestry. Here, Harold is shown swearing an oath to support William. He makes the promise with his hands on boxes containing holy relics – probably the bones of saints.

Activities

1. According to Source A, why should William have been crowned King of England instead of Harold?

2. a) What does William of Poitiers (Source C) think of Harold and his supporters?

   b) Why do you think he describes them in this way?

3. Why do you think the Bayeux Tapestry makes a point of showing Harold swearing an oath on the bones of saints? (Source B)

4. Why do you think that English sources such as the *Anglo-Saxon Chronicle* do not mention Edward's promise or Harold's oath?

5. a) How does Source C disagree with Source A on the previous page?

   b) What reasons could there be for these differences?

Checklist

- When Edward the Confessor died Harold Godwine became King of England.

- William, Duke of Normandy, thought that he should have been crowned king.

- Anglo-Saxon sources support Harold's claim to the throne, Norman sources support William's claim.

- In 1066 William invaded England. He defeated the English and Harold was killed. William won the crown of England on the battlefield.

THE NORMAN CONQUEST

1066 Battle of Hastings. William is crowned king.

Rebellion put down in the south of England.

Rebellion in the north of England is crushed.

1070

1071 Hereward the Wake's rebellion is put down.

William orders the Normans to build a castle to protect his soldiers.

1080

William the Conqueror

1087 William the Conqueror dies. His son is crowned William II.

Themes

William was crowned King of England in London on Christmas Day, 1066. However, his conquest of England had only just begun.

Many people refused to accept William as king. It was their land – the Normans had no right to take it from them. Between 1066 and 1087 there were rebellions against Norman rule. The rebellions were crushed and the English defeated. By 1087 the Normans had taken control of the whole of England.

This chapter asks the following questions.

- How did the Normans take control of England?

- How did they keep control?

The Focus looks at a rebellion against the Normans in 1071. This is how the story might be reported in a modern newspaper.

Focus Activities

Read the passage opposite.

1. Why was it so difficult for the Normans to take control of Ely?
   Give as many reasons as you can.

2. To the Normans, Hereward was an outlaw and his followers rebels.
   How do you think the English saw Hereward?
   Explain your answer.

ENGLISH REBELLION CRUSHED

Major battle

Reports are just coming in of the defeat of the English rebels at Ely. We have not been allowed into the area but we are getting some details of a major sea and land battle.

The Wake

This latest rebellion has been one of the most difficult for King William to deal with. Little is known about the rebel leader, Hereward, but we hear many rumours. The English call him 'the Wake' because of his great powers of concentration and his watchfulness. This outlaw first started his career of violence and destruction when the Norman abbot, Turold, was sent by William to take over the monastery at Peterborough.

Hereward and his men attacked the monastery, setting fire to it and making off with much of its gold and silver. They claimed that this was to prevent it falling into Norman hands. The rebels then fled to the island of Ely.

Troops ordered in

William at once ordered his troops into the area. The island of Ely, surrounded by water and marshes, is dangerous for those who do not know the hidden pathways. An unknown number of Norman soldiers drowned after losing their way, or being ambushed by rebels. Cutting off food supplies did not work as the area is full of cattle, deer, goats, hares and other wildlife. The rebels, like the local people, had plenty to eat.

Witch fails

In a desperate attempt to defeat Hereward, William is said to have built a tower facing into the marshes. In it he put a witch to hurl spells and curses at the rebels. A spokesman has refused to say anything about the story that Hereward burnt the tower – and the witch!

Rebels defeated

The breakthrough came when the Normans built a pathway across the marsh. Once on the island they quickly defeated the English rebels. King William now controls this part of England.

A 19th century artist's impression of Hereward attacking a Norman castle

Taking control

William brought barons – important and powerful men – with him from Normandy. They had already helped him invade England and defeat Harold. Now they helped him take control of the rest of the country.

The Normans quickly built castles in many parts of the kingdom to protect themselves from attacks by the English. From these castles the barons and their knights (soldiers) went out and put down rebellions. As Sources A and B show, they sometimes did this very violently.

Source A Putting down a rebellion

William killed many people. He destroyed the homes of others and burned them all to ashes. In his anger he ordered that all crops, herds of sheep and cattle, people's belongings and food be collected up and burned. As a result more than 100,000 Christian people, young and old, died of hunger.

Orderic Vitalis, 'Ecclesiastical History', 1123

Source B

Norman soldiers setting fire to an English house

Bayeux Tapestry

Activities

1. Study Sources A and B.
   a) In what way is Source B similar to Source A?
   b) Does this mean that what Source A says is more likely to be true? Explain your answer.
   c) Why do you think William took such tough action against the English?

2. Look at Source C.
   a) Draw and label a ground plan of a motte and bailey castle.
   b) Why did the Normans build castles?
   c) Why do you think these castles were first built in wood and later rebuilt in stone?

Source C An early motte and bailey castle

Keep – wooden tower to protect those in the castle if the enemy got into the bailey

Motte – high mound of earth from which the enemy could be watched

Bailey – courtyard for soldiers' homes, animals, barns and blacksmith's workshop

Ditch and fences – to protect the bailey from attack

Hundreds of these castles were built in wood by the Normans. Many were later rebuilt in stone.

The church

The church played an important part in the Norman conquest. The bishops who were in charge of the church were powerful men. William therefore chose men who would support him to be bishops.

These bishops then replaced many English priests with Norman priests. After the local lord the priest was the most important person in the village. People listened to what he said. So, if the priest said that William was a good king who ruled with God's blessing, then people might be more likely to accept his rule.

The Normans not only replaced English churchmen, they also replaced English churches, rebuilding them in the Norman style.

Source A	Bishops		
Date	English Bishops	Norman Bishops	Total
1066	16	0	16
1080	1	15	16

Michael Wood, 'Domesday', 1986

Source B   An English church

A small wooden church built in the 9th century at Greensted in Essex

Activities

1. In what way does Source A show how William made sure that the church would support him?

2. Look at Sources B and C.

   a) In what ways is Iffley church different from Greensted church?

   b) The following is a list of possible reasons why the Normans rebuilt many English churches. Write them out in order with the most likely reason first.

      - English churches were often made of wood and needed rebuilding.

      - The Normans wanted to get rid of anything that reminded people of England before 1066.

      - The Normans wanted to show who was now in charge.

      - The Normans preferred their own design of church.

   c) Explain why you have put them in this order.

Source C   A Norman church

A church rebuilt by the Normans at Iffley near Oxford

The feudal system

'What we want is land!' said the Norman barons. Land meant power and wealth. This was the reward the Normans demanded for conquering England. The land had been held by English earls. Many had died at the Battle of Hastings, some were killed or defeated in rebellions, some fled abroad. By the end of William's reign Normans held most of the land in England.

William used land to help him control England. The way land was held is known as the **feudal system**. It worked like this.

- All the land in England belonged to the king. He kept some for his own use and divided the rest between his 'tenants-in-chief' – the barons and bishops. In return for the land they and their knights fought for the king. They also made a promise to obey the king at all times.

- The barons and bishops kept some of this land for their own use and divided the rest between their 'sub-tenants' – the knights. In return for their land the knights and their villagers fought for their baron or bishop. They also promised to obey him.

- The knights kept some of this land for their own use and divided the rest between their 'tenants' – the villagers. In return for the land the villagers did a number of days work on the knight's land, paid taxes and promised to obey him.

Apart from the king everyone had a lord. This was the person from whom they held land and whom they promised to obey.

Source A   The feudal system

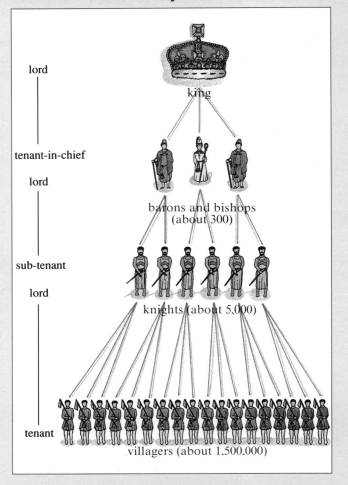

lord — king

tenant-in-chief
lord — barons and bishops (about 300)

sub-tenant
lord — knights (about 5,000)

tenant — villagers (about 1,500,000)

Source B   The village of Knebworth

Eudo FitzHubert holds Knebworth and Humphrey holds it from him. There is enough land for 12 ploughs *(a way of measuring land)*. The lord has enough land for 4 ploughs and 24 villagers have enough for 8 ploughs between them.

'Domesday Book', 1086

Activities

1. 'In the Middle Ages everyone had their place in life.'
   Explain this statement using Source A.

2. Copy out the table below and fill in the blanks with information from Source B. When completed it will show how the feudal system worked in one village.

   Tenant-in-chief – _____

   Sub-tenant – _____

   Number of villagers – _____

Land was very important in the Middle Ages. People needed it to grow food to feed their families. It also brought wealth to lords. Villagers had to pay taxes, like those shown in Source D, to their lords. Sometimes these taxes were paid with money, more often with goods that had been produced on the land.

Lords were powerful men. The more land they held the more powerful they were. If people disobeyed their lord or rebelled against him he could throw them off the land. This could happen to barons, bishops, knights or villagers.

Source C   Some feudal taxes

Villagers pay taxes to the lord.

Heriot	– a tax paid to the lord when people took over land after the death of their father.
Merchet	– a tax paid to the lord by a father when his daughter married.
Christmas	– each villager gave the lord a goose.
Easter	– each villager gave the lord some eggs.

Source D   Norman kings and their descendants

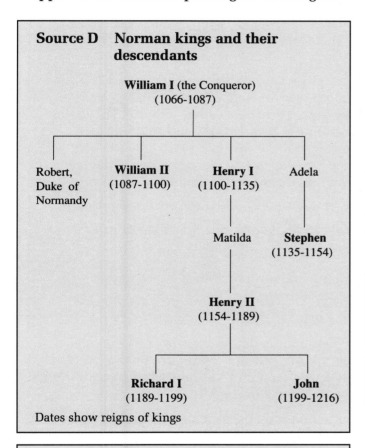

Dates show reigns of kings

Source E   Obeying the lord

I will be your man from this day onwards. I shall be true and faithful to you for the lands I hold from you.

'Oath of Allegiance', 11th century

3. a) Who had more power – a baron or a knight? Why?

b) How did holding land give people power?

4. Lords were not only powerful, they were also rich. Where did their wealth come from?

5. Study Source E. How did this promise help the Normans keep control of England?

6. How does Source D show the success of the Norman conquest?

Checklist

- Norman barons and knights helped William put down English rebellions.

- Castles were built to protect the barons and knights. They used them as bases from which they could control the surrounding area.

- William used the church and the feudal system to keep control over the kingdom.

4 THE VILLAGE

A lord and his lady go hunting

A woodcutter and herdsman

Haymaking

In medieval times England was a land of small villages. Most people worked on the land. Life was hard. The peasants usually managed to produce just enough to keep themselves alive. But if there was a bad harvest they could starve to death in the following winter.

Much of the land in the village was held by the lord of the manor – usually a knight. Most of the villagers were peasants called villeins. They held small amounts of the lord's land for their own use in return for obeying the lord and working his land for him. A few were freemen. They held their own land and were not tied to the lord.

This chapter looks at the following questions.

- What kind of work did the villagers do?
- What did the village produce?
- What work was done for the lord of the manor?
- How was village life organised?

We begin with a day in the life of Alwin, an elderly villein. Peasants could not read or write. The diary is based on descriptions of peasant life written by monks in the Middle Ages.

Focus Activities

Read the passage opposite.

1. A traveller comes to stay in the village. He asks Alwin what is wrong with his life and how it might be improved. What do you think Alwin would reply?

2. Alwin lives in fear of his lord. Why?

3. Why is the Focus called 'Diary of a Nobody'?

The Diary of a Nobody

I don't know why I write in this diary – every day's the same at this time of year. Up at the crack of dawn – well, before it really, shuffling round in the dark and cold. The fire always goes out hours before – not that we could get enough wood to keep it going through the night anyway. Then I stuff some straw into my wooden clogs to keep my feet warm – it's been frosty the last few days and the ground's cold and hard.

I grab the last of the stale bread and wash it down with some water, or ale if I'm lucky, then it's out into the fields to see whether I can get on with the ploughing today. It was too cold yesterday and my hands went numb repairing the thatch on the cottage, so I came inside and put a new handle on my sickle. I know I won't need it for a few months – haven't even planted the seeds yet – but I won't have time later on in the year for jobs like that.

I don't like the look of the milk cow, she's getting thin and the milk's just about dried up. If I can't get any more food for her I'm afraid she won't last till the grass grows again in spring. I know she's warm and comfortable inside here with us, and she helps to keep us warm, too, but she's even hungrier than we are.

The stew is getting thinner every day. Wife says we're almost out of meat. If there'd been more rain last summer there would have been more grass on the common for the animals. Then there would have been more meat on them in the autumn when we slaughtered them and salted the meat. I'm frightened that one of my sons will become desperate enough to set traps for rabbits. If he's caught my lord will deal with him very harshly for taking his game.

Not being free makes the work seem so much harder. I have to spend three days a week working for my lord. I dare not refuse. If I did he'd throw me off my land and where would I be then?

I really begin to feel my age at this time of the year. If only the weather would improve.

Keeping warm

The milk cow

Work in the village

The pictures on these two pages show scenes from village life. Most of the villagers were farmers. They grew wheat, barley, oats, rye and fruit and vegetables. They kept cows, pigs, sheep, goats and chickens. Some of the villagers had other jobs such as the carpenter, the blacksmith and the miller.

Most of the things people needed were produced in the village. In other words the village was largely self-sufficient.

Source A

The carpenter

Source B

The blacksmith at work in the smithy

The pictures show that people often worked together – they cooperated. Every member of the family helped, from the youngest to the oldest. At certain times of the year, for example at harvest, many of the villagers worked together.

Food for animals was scarce in the winter and so in the autumn most were killed and their meat was salted to preserve it. What little could not be used was burned on 'bonefires' at Hallow E'en.

Source C

Harrowing – breaking up the soil after ploughing and covering the seeds. The man on the left is scaring birds.

Source D

Taking grain to the miller

Source E

Harvesting

Activities

1. Choose three of the sources and use them to show how people in the village cooperated.

2. Why do you think that the blacksmith, the miller and the carpenter were important to village life?

3. Women played a vital part in producing things that the villagers needed. Use Sources D, E, F and G to explain how. Why was this work so important?

4. The medieval village was largely self-sufficient.

   a) What does this mean?

   b) Make a list of the things produced by the villagers.

5. You are a farmer in the Middle Ages. Describe the main jobs that have to be done throughout the year.

Source F

Slaughtering cattle

Source G

Spinning wool

Source H

Threshing – beating out and separating the grain – and winnowing – blowing the chaff (husks) from the grain

Working for the lord

'It's hard work all right, sir, because I'm not free', says the ploughman in Source C. As a villein he had to obey his lord and do work for him. He needed his permission to travel outside the village and to get married. His grain had to be ground at the lord's mill. In return for his land a villein had to do work service on the lord's land, give him some of the food he produced and make payments of money to the lord.

All villagers, including villeins, had to give one tenth of everything they produced to the church. This was known as the tithe and the food was stored in the village tithebarn (Source B).

As the title of the Focus suggests villeins were 'nobodies'. With only small plots of land they were poor and powerless.

Source A   The shepherd

Shepherd: 'At daybreak I drive the sheep to their pasture. I watch over them with my dogs in both hot and cold weather to stop wolves carrying them off. Twice a day, I lead them back to the sheepfolds and milk them. I stay with them in the folds and make cheese and butter. I am faithful to my lord.'

'The Colloquies of Aelfric', 989-1002

Source B   A tithebarn

Source C   The ploughman

Master: 'What have you to say, ploughman? Tell me how you go about your work.'

Ploughman: 'Oh I work very hard indeed, sir. Every day at the crack of dawn I have to drive the oxen out of the field and yoke them to the plough. I would never dare scive at home, no matter how bad the winter weather. I'm too frightened of my lord for that. No, once I've yoked the oxen and fastened the share and coulter to the plough, I must plough a full acre or more every day.'

Master: 'Oh my, it sounds like hard work.'

Ploughman: 'It's hard work all right, sir, because I'm not free.'

'The Colloquies of Aelfric', 989-1002

Source D

The lord's reeve (foreman) directing the harvest

Activities

1. Study Sources A and C.
   a) What difference would being free make to the ploughman?
   b) What do you think the shepherd means when he says, 'I am faithful to my lord'?

2. The tithebarn shown in Source B is very large. What does this suggest about the problems faced by villagers struggling to feed their families?

3. Study Sources D and E.
   a) Why would the reeve keep a watchful eye on villeins doing work service?
   b) Why would most villeins do their work service properly?

4. Read sources F and G. Why do you think the villagers often grumbled about their work service and payments to the lord?

Source E   Punishments

William Jordan is punished because he ploughed the lord's land badly. Fined 6 pence. Elias of Streatham is punished for not doing his work service in the autumn. Fined 6 pence.

'Tooting Manorial Court Roll', October 1247

Source F   Death duty

John Geiard had very little when he died. In order for his nine year old son to take over the land he farmed, a death duty of two cows and two horses had to be paid to the lord. This left the boy and his family with a plough, a cart, a brass pot and dish and a few farming tools.

Michael Wood, 'Domesday', 1986

Source G   Work service

The villeins work three days a week up to the feast of St Peter in August and then up to Michaelmas (29th September) every day. Each villein should plough one acre at the winter ploughing and one acre at the spring, and separate the seed from the chaff at the lord's barn, and sow it. They must give the lord 5 shillings at Christmas and 5 shillings at Easter and 32 pence at St Peter's feast. And Agemund the miller pays 26 shillings for his mill. And all the villeins must give 32 hens at Christmas.

'The Black Book of Peterborough', c.1125

Village life

It was easy to tell who was who in a medieval village. The large manor house in its own grounds belonged to the lord. The villeins lived in thatched huts grouped round the village green. Most had small gardens in which they grew fruit and vegetables for their families.

Around the village there were usually three large fields each divided into long strips. A villein would farm some strips in each of the three fields. This meant that no one got all the good or bad land.

Each year one of the fields was left fallow – no crops were grown and farm animals were left to manure it. This gave the soil a chance to get its goodness back. The other two fields were sown with grain crops – usually wheat for bread or barley for beer (Source B).

Strip farming meant that villeins had to work together at certain times of the year. A whole field had to be sown at once since the seeds blew from one strip to another. All the strips had to be harvested at the same time since harvesting only one might damage crops in the next strip.

Most villeins had chickens and a cow and many had sheep, goats, oxen and pigs. The chickens scratched round the huts and the animals grazed on the fallow field and common land that surrounded the village. Villagers also collected firewood from the common land.

Source A   A reconstruction of a medieval village

Around their huts the villeins had gardens in which they grew peas, beans, cabbages, leeks, onions, herbs, apples, pears, plums and cherries.

Activities

1. Why was crop rotation used? (Source B)

2. Use the information in this section to list as many reasons as you can why the villeins worked together to farm their land.

3. a) Why do you think the villeins had gardens when the fields and animals took up so much of their time?

   b) What foods that you eat regularly are not mentioned in this section? Can you suggest reasons for this?

4. You are writing a guide to England in the Middle Ages for foreign visitors. Give a short description of a medieval village.

Source B   Crop rotation

Year	West field	East field	South field
1	Fallow	Wheat	Barley
2	Barley	Fallow	Wheat
3	Wheat	Barley	Fallow

A three year plan for planting crops

Source C   The dishonest villein

If I ploughed I would steal a foot of land from my neighbour; and if I harvested I would reach across into my neighbour's ground.

William Langland, 'Piers Plowman', 1377-79

Source D   Plan of a medieval village

west field

east field

village green

villeins' huts
and gardens

priest's house

church

south field

lord's water mill

tithebarn

barn

stream

manor house

workshops for carpenter
and blacksmith

commons

Checklist

- Villages were largely self-sufficient. Most of what was needed was produced in the village.

- Much of the land in the village was held by the lord of the manor. Villeins were granted small amounts of his land for their own use.

- In return they obeyed their lord, worked on his land and gave him money and things they produced.

- Farmland was divided into strips. Each villein had a number of strips spread over three large fields.

- The villeins worked together to plough and harvest their strips.

- Around the village centre were the villeins' huts and gardens. The lord of the manor lived in a large house on the edge of the village.

5 TOWNS AND TRADE

John Hooker's map of Exeter. Although drawn in 1587 it shows what Exeter was like in the Middle Ages.

The Shambles, York. This street was built in the Middle Ages. It gives a good idea of what a medieval street looked like.

Themes

Although most people lived in the countryside in tiny villages, many new towns grew up in the Middle Ages. Compared to today medieval towns were small and crowded. In the 15th century London had a population of only 40-50,000. Most country towns had no more than 500. They were smelly and dirty places. Rubbish was dumped in the streets. There were no drains and farm animals wandered freely round the narrow alleyways.

They were also very busy places. Although most medieval townspeople still worked the land they spent more and more time making and selling things.

Medieval towns grew up around markets. They were centres of trade – places where people came to buy and sell goods. This chapter asks the following questions.

- How did towns grow up?
- How was buying and selling organised?
- What did craftsmen make and how were they organised?

We start with a description of a court in a medieval town. The court is deciding on the punishment for a trader who has sold poor quality goods.

Focus Activities

Read the passage opposite.

1. Why did towns have Pie Powder Courts?

2. Pie Powder Courts tried to make the punishment fit the crime. What punishments would you suggest for:
   - a potter who sold cracked jugs
   - a tailor who sold clothes which came apart at the seams
   - a fishmonger who sold rotten fish
   - a haberdasher who sold shoelaces which snapped?

Court of Pie Powder

> The name 'Pie Powder' comes from the French words 'pieds poudrés' meaning 'dusty feet' – people often walked miles to the town along dusty tracks.

Steward *(person who organised the court):*

Ladies and gentlemen, the Court of Pie Powder for Salisbury is about to begin.

We have called you to this court to make an important decision. Six of you are traders and six of you are customers. Your job is to decide whether this wine merchant is guilty or not guilty of selling poor quality wine. As you know the market is over tomorrow so a decision must be reached quickly. People must see that we run the market fairly. If they think a tradesman is dishonest they will not come back and that will be bad for all of us.

The accused is John Penrose. The constable arrested him after complaints about his red wine. His customers claim that it is so bad as to be undrinkable. Indeed one goes so far as to describe it as vinegar! Try some yourselves.

Now ladies and gentlemen, what is your verdict?

Spokesman:

Guilty! This wine is really awful.

Steward:

What shall his punishment be? Shall he have his hands and neck locked into the pillory, or his ankles put in the stocks, so that everyone can make fun of him and throw rotten eggs and vegetables at him? Or can you suggest a more suitable punishment?

Spokesman:

We sentence John Penrose to drink this cask of wine himself and to have the rest of his wine poured over his head. This punishment is to be carried out in the market place in front of everyone.

Stocks in the market square at Ripley, North Yorkshire

How towns grew

Not all markets became towns. Those that did usually grew up:

- where main roads crossed
- near a bridge over a river
- by a castle or monastery.

These places usually had a number of things in common – they were easy to get to, they were meeting places, people often lived nearby.

As more people came to the markets, shops were built for traders and workshops for craftsmen. Inns were built for travelling merchants who needed food and drink and a place to stay. Houses were built for people in the town to live in. Most towns grew up in this way.

Source A   Launceston, Cornwall

Source B   Stamford, Lincolnshire

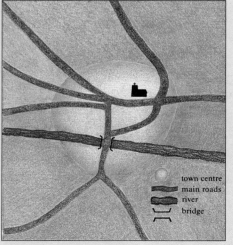

town centre
main roads
river
bridge

Activities

1. Study Sources A and B then copy and complete the table below.

	Reason(s) why the town grew
Launceston	
Stamford	

2. The map opposite shows *five* possible sites for a town.
   a) List them in order with the best site first.
   b) Explain your reasons for deciding which site is best.

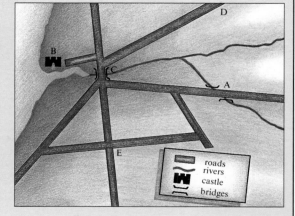

roads
rivers
castle
bridges

Towns grew up on land held by a lord. The townspeople had to work the lord's land just like the villagers. They also had to pay taxes on goods sold in the market. As the towns grew, traders and craftsmen wanted to spend more time making and selling goods. They made agreements with their lord to pay rent for their land rather than doing work service for him. These agreements were known as charters and allowed people to make their own decisions about running the town.

Once they had a charter the local traders were free from the taxes that traders from outside the town had to pay to sell their goods in the market.

Lords were usually happy to agree to charters. The townspeople had to pay the lord money for the charter and rents made up for the taxes and work service the lord lost.

Towns with charters were known as boroughs and the people that lived in them were called burgesses.

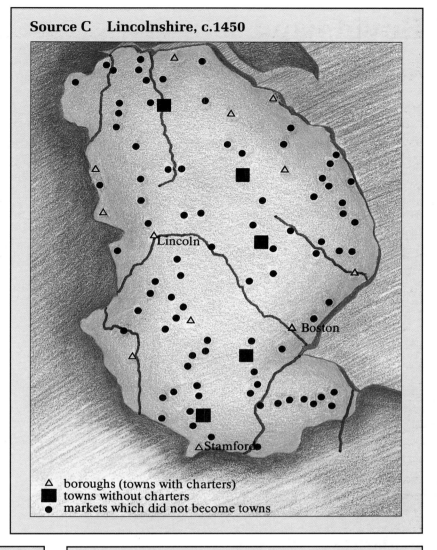

Source C   Lincolnshire, c.1450

Lincoln

Boston

Stamford

△ boroughs (towns with charters)
■ towns without charters
● markets which did not become towns

Source D   Charters

The burgesses may:

1. **rent land** for their own use without working for the lord;

2. **hold markets** every week without paying taxes to the lord;

3. **hold fairs** every year;

4. have the **right of assize** – to set a fixed price for goods sold at the market;

5. **hold courts** to punish traders who break the rules of the market;

6. have the **right of gallows** – to punish criminals by hanging.

Charters like this were granted to many towns during the Middle Ages.

---

3. a) Copy and complete the table below using information from Source C.

Lincolnshire	Number
Markets which did not become towns	
Towns without charters	
Boroughs	

b) Why did so many towns become boroughs? Think of the advantages of having a charter to:

– the townspeople

– the lord.

Buying and selling

In most towns, markets were held two or three times a week. People from nearby villages came to sell goods they had produced themselves – milk, eggs, meat and vegetables. They bought things they could not make such as knives, pots and pans.

On market days traders set up stalls rather like those seen in street markets today. Some sold food. Others sold clothes, shoes, gloves, pottery and many other things. In small towns traders set up their stalls in the town centre at a place usually marked by a stone cross – the market cross. In larger towns different parts of the town were used by traders selling the same thing. For example all the bakers might be in the same street – Bread Street.

As towns grew bigger some traders built shops. Shops had several advantages. Traders did not have to pack away at the end of each day. It was more difficult for thieves to steal from a shop. Traders and their goods were protected from bad weather, and goods could be sold on days when the market was not held.

Source B   Market stalls around a town wall

Activities

1. Study Source A.

    a) Whereabouts in London would you have gone if you wanted to buy:
    (i) wine, (ii) pigs?

    b) What traders might you have expected to find in the following streets:

    Cutler Street, Brewhouse Lane, Silver Street, Coopers Lane, Mercers Row, Vine Street, Tanners Lane, Bow Lane, Threadneedle Street?

    You will probably need a dictionary for this question.

    c) What advantages might there be in having all traders selling the same thing close to each other for:
    (i) the customers, (ii) the traders?

2. Look at Source B.

    a) Describe what is happening in the picture.

    b) What are the differences between the market stalls shown and a modern shop?

    c) What advantages does a modern shop have over these stalls?

Fairs were special occasions. They were held only once or twice a year and might last as long as a fortnight. People came from all over the area to buy and sell, to be entertained, to eat and drink and to meet old friends. Jugglers, acrobats, fire eaters and musicians performed in the streets and plays were put on in the market place. Crowds of excited people filled the town.

Apart from the usual market traders, merchants brought goods from other parts of the country. Many sold wool which was produced in large amounts in the Middle Ages. Wool was cheap so villagers and poor townspeople bought it to make clothes. Some merchants brought exotic goods from other countries – fine silk and furs, expensive wine and spices. Only rich people could afford to buy these goods.

Source C   Where goods were produced

In other countries
linen
timber
wine
spices
silk
furs
canvas
hawks
fruit
rope

In England
wool
iron
lead
salt
leather
fish
grain
farm animals

△ Hull
△ Boston
△ Bristol
△ London
▲ ports

Source D   Goods for sale at Boston Fair, c.1250

wool	leather	fish
wine	silk	grain
lead	farm animals	hawks
canvas	spices	furs

Source E   Rich and poor

The poor wore clothes made of wool. Leather was used to make belts and pouches.

The rich wore clothes made of silk. Furs were used to line their clothes.

3. Study Sources C and D.

   a) Which of the goods on sale at Boston Fair were produced in:

      – England

      – other countries?

   b) Why do you think Boston was a good place to go if you wanted to buy goods from other countries?

4. Using Source E say which of the goods on sale at Boston Fair might be bought by:

   – the rich

   – the poor?

   Explain your answer.

5. You are twelve years old and this is your first visit to the fair. It is the most exciting day of your life – strange sounds, sights and smells. Describe your visit.

Crafts and guilds

Many of the goods sold at markets and fairs were produced by craftsmen. They were made by hand using tools such as hammers and chisels. Making goods by hand is known as craftwork. The bigger a town grew the more crafts there were. As Source A shows, people's names can often tell us what was made.

Most craftsmen worked in small workshops. There was a master craftsman who was in charge, one or two journeymen (paid workers) and one or two apprentices (trainees). Most workshops were in the centre of towns. The craftsmen sold their goods from stalls in front of their workshops. Other craftsmen, like carpenters and stonemasons, built houses and shops.

Source A   Craftsmen in Coventry

Henry the lead-beater	Robert the cook
Hugh the carpenter	Thomas the painter
Hugh the hosier	William the builder
John the cordwainer	William the butter-maker
John the thatcher	William the cutler
Pagan the miller	William the belt-maker
Ralph the weaver	William the skinner
Richard the combere	Richard the saddler
Robert the baker	

combere – prepared wool for clothmaking
cordwainer – made boots
cutler – made knives
hosier – made stockings and socks
skinner – took skins off animals
thatcher – made house roofs from straw or reeds
weaver – made cloth

'Warwickshire Feet of Fines', 1250-1340

Source B   Making glass

The various stages in making glass are shown, from digging the sand from which glass is made, through heating it in coal-burning ovens, to blowing it into shape and checking the finished object for faults.

Activities

1. Study Source A.

   a) Copy and complete the table below. Place the name of each craftsman under the correct heading.

Building trades	Making things to wear	Making things to eat	Other
	Ralph the weaver		

   b) Design a poster advertising Coventry. You will need to tell people what goods are made there and that Coventry's craftsmen make everything they need. Remember that most people could not read so you will need to use pictures as well as words.

2. Look at Source B.

   a) Describe each stage of glass making.

   b) Why do you think glass workshops were usually on the edge of towns rather than in the centre? Remember that most houses in medieval times were built of wood and had thatched roofs.

3. Some people have surnames which suggest they have an ancestor who was a craftsman. Make a list of people in your school with names like this.

As towns grew, craftsmen worried that they might lose customers to others who sold cheaper but poorer quality goods. If there were too many potters, shoemakers or hat makers then they might not be able to earn enough to live on. If the goods they made were of poor quality then the whole craft might get a bad name.

Craftsmen formed themselves into clubs known as guilds. Only members were allowed to work at the craft. The guilds made rules about the quality and price of goods and the training and qualifications of members. Master craftsmen took on apprentices and taught them their skills. After seven years training they were given a test (see Source D). If they passed they could become masters too. If they could not afford to pay the fee to the guild to set up their own workshop, they became journeymen working for other masters while they saved up. Guilds also looked after their members when they were sick or too old to work.

Source D   Making a 'masterpiece'

After seven years training an apprentice had to prove his skill by making a piece for his master to show the high standard of his work.

Source C   Guild rules

Poor workmanship will be punished by a fine and having all goods confiscated.
Shoemakers' Guild, Chester

No-one shall make or sell hats within the city unless he is a burgess of the city.
Hatmakers' Guild, London

If the threads of the cloth are too far apart, the cloth and the tools used will be burned.
Weavers' Guild, Bristol

If by chance any member of the guild shall become poor through old age, accident or sickness, then he shall have 7 pence (3p) from the guild every week.
Tanners' Guild (leather workers), London

4. Why do you think the word 'masterpiece' was used (Source D)?

5. Why was it so important in medieval times for guilds to give money to members who could not work because of old age, sickness or accident? Think how such people would manage today.

6. You are setting up a medieval craft guild – you might choose shoemakers, potters or dressmakers. Use the information on this page to decide the rules of the guild and how you will make sure your members obey them.

Checklist

- Towns grew up around busy markets where people came to buy and sell goods.
- Townspeople often made agreements with their lord which allowed them to make decisions about the way towns were run.
- Towns became centres of trade where people could buy goods from different parts of England and from other countries.
- Craftsmen in towns made many of the things people needed.
- Craftsmen set up guilds which made rules about the quality and price of goods and the training of their members.

THE CHURCH

The time and money spent on impressive buildings like Canterbury Cathedral show how important religion was to people in the Middle Ages.

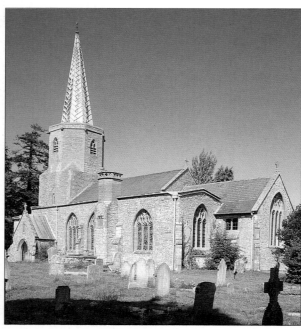

Every village had its own church – much smaller than a cathedral. This church is in the village of Pitminster in Somerset.

Themes

In the Middle Ages the church was rich and powerful. It played an important part in everybody's lives from the king down to the poorest villager. It was the centre of the community, taking care of people in life and looking after their souls when they died. In return, the church demanded respect, obedience to the will of God and one tenth of everybody's income – a 'tithe'.

This did not mean that people always got on well with the church. Kings, in particular, frequently argued with important churchmen such as the pope and the Archbishop of Canterbury.

This chapter looks at the following questions.

- Why was the church so powerful?
- What part did the church play in the lives of ordinary people?
- Why did people become monks and nuns?

We begin by looking at what happened when Henry II quarrelled with the Archbishop of Canterbury, Thomas Becket. The Focus is based on an eye-witness account by Edward Grim – an old monk.

Focus Activities

Read the passage opposite.

1. Why do you think Thomas refused to take Edward Grim's advice and flee from the cathedral?

2. Why did Grim think that the cross might stop the knights from murdering Thomas?

3. Why did Henry order the monks to whip him in front of Thomas's tomb?

Murder in the Cathedral

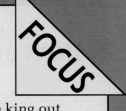

I warned the archbishop, you know. I said that if he threw those bishops who supported the king out of the church, the king would be furious – and we all know about his temper! Thomas took no notice. He said that the church had to come before the king. God was more important than Henry II.

It was only a few days after Christmas. We were getting ready for evening service when four knights arrived. Believing they were carrying out the king's wishes, they forced their way in and told Thomas to leave the country. He refused saying, 'If you threatened me with all the swords in England you could not stop me doing my duty to God'.

The knights left but we saw them outside putting on their armour. We tried to persuade Thomas to flee, but he calmly went ahead with the evening service, leading the procession into the cathedral. He wouldn't even let us bolt the door.

Suddenly the knights burst in. 'Where is the man who has turned against the king?' one shouted. Thomas answered quietly, 'I'm here – I have not turned against the king, I am just a priest doing God's will. What do you want?' 'Your death!' came the reply and Reginald FitzUrse, one of the knights, lifted up his sword. I rushed forward with a cross to protect Thomas, but the sword came down on my arm cutting it almost to the bone. I fell, bleeding and helpless. A second knight, William de Tracy, hit Thomas on the head with his sword. As he fell to his knees a third knight, Richard le Breton, struck him so hard that he cut off the top of his head, spilling Thomas's brains on the floor and breaking his sword.

Many people were angry with Henry II and blamed him for Thomas's death. Henry said he was sorry. To make his sorrow clear to everybody he ordered us to whip him as he knelt before Thomas's tomb. He needed to do this to make his peace with the church.

Thomas has now been made a saint. Hundreds come to his tomb every year. Several say there have been miracles after their visits – one young man claims he was cured of leprosy, a very serious disease.

Edward Grim tries to protect Thomas Becket with a cross.

Power and wealth

Archbishops and bishops were important – people listened to them and took their advice. This was partly because they were rich and powerful. The church held about a third of the land in England. The bishops, like the barons, were the king's tenants-in-chief.

The bishops and other important churchmen were usually well-educated men – they could read and write, something not many kings could do. They also came from noble families and were used to dealing with important people. This made them very useful to the king. They advised him, wrote important documents and represented him on trips abroad.

Henry II made a churchman, Thomas Becket, Chancellor of England. Becket was his friend – he was now his chief adviser. He supported the king and helped him to control the barons. Henry then made him Archbishop of Canterbury, hoping that Becket would control the church too. But things did not work out as Henry had planned.

The church had its own courts for priests who broke the law. They gave much lighter punishments than Henry's courts. A priest who murdered someone would be thrown out of the church, but anyone else would be hanged for this crime. Henry wanted criminals found guilty in church courts to be handed over to the king's courts for punishment. Thomas refused. As archbishop he defended the church courts. Even after Becket's death Henry failed to get his own way.

Activities

1. How can we tell from Source A that Thomas was very wealthy?

2. How do Sources A and B show the power of churchmen in the Middle Ages?

Source A   Becket as chancellor

As Chancellor of England, Becket is the next most important person to the king. Everything is done with the chancellor's advice. When Becket crosses the English channel he never has less than six ships. Every day he gives away valuable presents of horses, birds, clothes, gold and silver dishes and money. When the day's work is over Thomas and the king relax together. They play like two young boys.

William FitzStephen, c.1170

Source B   A coronation

A king had to be crowned by an archbishop. Archbishops could refuse to crown kings.

Look at the skyline of London today – banks, building societies, office blocks, department stores, universities, museums, government buildings and the occasional church. In the Middle Ages churches towered above the city, dominating the skyline. In towns and villages all over the country the biggest and most important buildings were the churches. They took years to build and cost vast amounts of money. Hardly a building came close to them in size, magnificence and splendour. They stood as evidence of the power and wealth of the church.

Source C

The London skyline in the Middle Ages

The London skyline today

Source D   The nave of Exeter cathedral

3. Look at Source C.

   a) What are the differences between the London skyline today and in the Middle Ages?

   b) What does this tell us about the church in the Middle Ages?

   c) What does it tell us about how people's attitude to life may have changed since the Middle Ages?

4. You have just visited Exeter cathedral (Source D). Write a letter to a friend describing it. Mention its size, the hand-carved stonework and the time and care which must have been spent building this church.

Church and people

Religion was very important to people in the Middle Ages. Almost everyone believed in God, Jesus, the saints and the power of the pope who was head of the church. Heaven and hell were real places and the best way to make sure you went to heaven was to lead a good life and obey the teachings of the church.

People in medieval times used religion to explain things. Sickness or bad harvests were punishments from God, the death of a baby was God's will. Heaven was a reward for a good life and made up for suffering on earth.

Source A   A 'doom painting'

Pictures like this were painted on the walls of village churches. They showed the joys of heaven and the horrors of hell.

After the lord of the manor, the priest was the most important person in the village. On Sundays he told people about the joys of heaven and the horrors of hell. His words were backed up by 'doom paintings' on the walls of village churches (Source A).

Activities

1. Study Sources A and B.

   a) Explain in your own words what is happening in the picture (Source A).

   b) What effect do you think pictures like Source A and sermons like Source B would have on medieval people?

   c) Why did pictures play such an important part in explaining ideas about religion to people in the Middle Ages?

2. Use Source B to draw your own 'doom painting'.

Source B   A sermon

And God let Paul see what Hell was like. He saw those who had been wicked being tortured on burning trees. They were hung by their feet, or hands, or hair, or neck, or tongue or arm. There was a furnace with seven huge flames and many of the wicked were punished in it. It was kept for the souls of those who were never sorry for their wickedness.

We ought to be frightened of Hell, where there is everlasting misery. There is a flaming wheel which a devil turns a thousand times a day and at each turn a thousand souls are burnt on it. And there is a horrible river, full of fish-like monsters which gobble up the souls of the wicked, who get what they deserve. But over the river there is a bridge and the souls of good people pass across the river without fear.

Bede, c.720

Every village had its church which was the centre of village life. Meetings were held there and the churchyard was often used for children's games in the summer evenings.

The village priest cared for people from the day they were born to the day they died. There were few schools or hospitals. Sources C-F show some of the things the priest did.

Source C

Baptising a baby

Source D

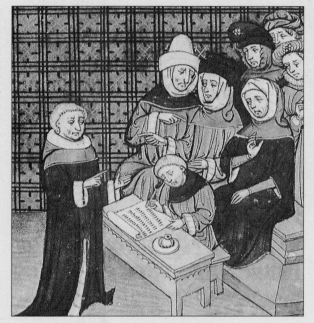

Teaching the son of a wealthy family

Source E

Treating a sick man

Source F

Burying the dead

3. Use Sources C-F to complete the following table:

What was done	Who did it in the Middle Ages	Who does it nowadays

4. Use Sources A-F to explain how important the priest was to people in the Middle Ages.

Monks and nuns

Many men and women became monks or nuns. They gave up everything to give their lives to God. This meant praying, working hard on the land and caring for others. Monks lived in monasteries and nuns lived in convents. Most monasteries and convents were small with only a few monks or nuns in each. Some monasteries, though, were much larger, like the one at Rievaulx shown in Source D. Monasteries like this were known as abbeys.

Monks and nuns often cut themselves off from the rest of the world, building monasteries and convents in quiet and lonely places far away from towns and villages. Life was not supposed to be easy. They had to obey rules like those in Source C. Church services were held at 2am, dawn, mid-morning, afternoon and in the evening. The monastery church was not heated, even in winter.

Source A   An artist's drawing of an abbey

Source B	A monk's timetable
2.0 am	Prayers in the abbey church
3.0 am	Back to bed in the dormitory
6.0 am	Get up at sunrise Prayers in the abbey church Breakfast of bread and ale in the refectory
7.0 am	Meeting in the chapter house to organise work for the day
8.0 am	Walk in the cloisters to relax and think
11.0 am	Prayers in the abbey church
12.0 noon	Main dinner eaten in the refectory
12.30 pm	Prayers in the abbey church
1.0 pm	Work at the farm or mill
6.0 pm	Prayers in the abbey church
7.0 pm	Supper in the refectory
8.0 pm	Prayers in the abbey church
9.0 pm	Bedtime in the dormitory

Activities

1. Copy the plan of an abbey shown below. Using Sources A and B label the places where the monks:
   - said their prayers
   - held their meetings
   - relaxed
   - ate their meals
   - slept.

   Use the names shown in Source A.

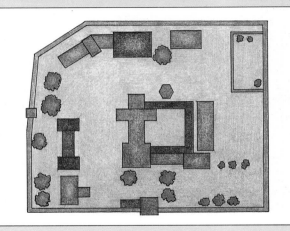

Source C   Rule of St Benedict

Monks must suffer like Christ did on earth if they are to be rewarded in heaven. To make sure of his reward a monk must promise:

- to spend his whole life working for God and praying

- to give all his belongings away to others

- to obey the abbot, the head of the monastery

- to wear a habit (monk's robe) and sandals

- to stay in the monastery until he dies

- not to marry.

St Benedict, 6th century

Source E

There is clear evidence that some of the nuns at Romsey bring birds, rabbits, hounds and other silly things to church and pay more attention to them than praying to God.

Letter from the Bishop of Winchester, 1387

Source D   The ruins of Rievaulx Abbey, Yorkshire

Here everything is peaceful and there is a wonderful quietness. We are free from all the noise and worry of the world. All the monks are very friendly and no one is selfish.

Walter Daniel, a monk at Rievaulx, c.1170

2. Study Sources C and D.

a) What reason does each suggest for people becoming monks?

b) Which reason do you think best explains why people became monks in the Middle Ages?

3. Were the nuns described in Source E as religious as St Benedict would have liked them to be? Explain your answer.

4. Use the sources in this section to make up a conversation between two boys. One wants to become a monk and the other tries to talk him out of it.

Checklist

- The church was wealthy. Bishops and abbots held large amounts of land. Many large and impressive churches were built.

- Church leaders played an important part in governing England.

- Religion was a part of everybody's life.

- The priest was an important person, caring for people in his town or village.

- Some people gave up everything to become monks or nuns, spending their lives working for God.

7 HENRY II AND GOVERNMENT

— 1135 Henry I dies. Stephen becomes king – start of civil war between Stephen and Matilda.

— 1154 Stephen dies. Henry of Anjou is crowned Henry II.

— 1170 Murder of Becket (see Chapter 6).

— 1189 Death of Henry II – his son is crowned Richard I.

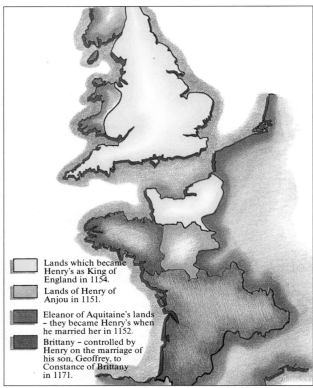

Lands which became Henry's as King of England in 1154.

Lands of Henry of Anjou in 1151.

Eleanor of Aquitaine's lands – they became Henry's when he married her in 1152.

Brittany – controlled by Henry on the marriage of his son, Geoffrey, to Constance of Brittany in 1171.

Henry II's lands

Themes

Henry of Anjou came to the throne of England as King Henry II after the death of Stephen in 1154. For nearly twenty years there had been civil war between Stephen and Henry's mother Matilda. The country was in ruins – villages destroyed and crops burned. Many of the barons were outside the king's control – they had captured his castles and tortured innocent people.

Henry had a difficult job ahead of him. He had to bring peace, force the barons to obey him and rule both England and his lands in France. Although he succeeded this did not mean he was a popular king. Henry had many enemies but most people respected him for his strength, determination, efficiency and fairness. When he died he passed on a peaceful and prosperous kingdom to his son Richard.

This chapter asks the following questions.

● How did Henry II rule his lands?

● Why did people obey him?

The Focus looks at the first year of Henry's reign. This is what a chronicler of the time might have thought about the new king.

Focus Activities

Read the passage opposite.

1. Why was it important for Henry II to defeat the barons and take control of the castles they had captured?

2. Imagine you are Hugh Mortimer. Write a letter to Henry II explaining why you refuse to give up your castles.

Review of the Year 1155

It's Christmas 1155 and just twelve months since Henry, Count of Anjou, arrived in England with his wife to be crowned king in Westminster Abbey.

Although only 21 years old he was already well known as a successful soldier and leader. After so many years of civil war in England – the result of a weak king whom the barons would not obey – what did the future hold? Many of us looked forward to having a new king to put an end to all the troubles affecting the country. But would the barons obey him?

Henry's first move was to order them to give up all of the castles that they had taken from King Stephen during the civil war – a brave step! Some of the barons were very powerful. Indeed William le Gros, the Earl of York, has been called 'more truly king than his master'. And it was William who refused to obey Henry. He had a lot of support from other barons and we all wondered what would happen.

Within a month of becoming king, Henry took an army to meet him. It didn't take William long to decide to give in. The young king certainly meant business!

Some barons thought they wouldn't have to give up castles because they'd been on Henry's mother's side in the civil war. Not a bit of it! Roger, Earl of Hereford, and Hugh Mortimer both found that Henry meant what he said. Roger was persuaded to give up his castles at Hereford and Gloucester. Hugh was not as sensible – he refused. So Henry attacked his castles and captured them one by one – Cleobury, Wigmore, Bridgnorth. Hugh had no choice but to surrender.

Other barons took a different way out. William Peverel fled abroad – well, he had been accused of poisoning another baron. Henry of Blois – King Stephen's brother and a powerful bishop – retired to the Abbey of Cluny in France. His castles were knocked down.

Henry has clearly won. Only one year into his reign and he is master of all his barons.

Henry II

Ruling an empire

By the time he died in 1189 King Henry II ruled an empire covering all of England, half of France and large parts of Wales and Scotland (see the map on page 40). He also laid claim to Ireland.

It was no easy matter to rule an empire as big as this. In a world without radio, telephone and television it was difficult for a ruler to know what was going on in all parts of his lands. Henry travelled great distances, staying with barons, keeping an eye on what was happening and letting his subjects know he was in charge.

To make sure that his orders were carried out efficiently Henry gathered trusted officials around him. They were known as the royal household. The most important officials of the household are shown in Source C. They travelled with the king on his journeys.

Source C The king's household

Main officials

Chancellor – in charge of people who wrote letters and sent out the king's orders. He was the only one allowed to use the king's official seal – the stamp which showed that documents were from the king.

Treasurer – looked after the king's money and valuable belongings. He was in charge of people who kept accounts so that the king always knew how much money he had.

Steward – in charge of the hall where the king and his advisers ate – he supervised cooks, butlers and other servants.

Chamberlain – in charge of the king's bedroom and personal belongings.

Source D

Worried that some neighbour would invade his lands Henry II put his closest friends in charge of Normandy.

'Chronicles of Ralph of Diceto', late 12th century

Source A

Since there were many things to do, Henry set sail from Ireland as it got dark and the next day arrived in Wales. From there he went straight to Portchester on the south coast of England where, getting on board a ship, he said goodbye to England and, after crossing the Channel, arrived in Normandy. When the King of France heard about this journey he said, 'At one moment the King of England is in Ireland, the next in England, the next in Normandy – he must fly rather than travel by horse or ship'.

'Chronicles of Ralph of Diceto', late 12th century

Source B A king on his travels

Activities

1. Using Sources A-D, explain the methods Henry II used to rule his lands.

2. The following comments were made about Henry II by people at the time.
   - 'He was generous to the poor.'
   - 'He listened carefully to advice.'
   - 'He was a good organiser.'
   - 'He never got tired.'
   Suggest how each of these comments helps to explain why Henry was a successful king.

Law and order

At the start of Henry's reign the country was in disorder. The barons had their own law courts but they were more interested in making money from them than seeing that people got a fair trial. Their courts punished people by large fines that went straight into the barons' pockets. There were stories of innocent people being fined or even executed – their land and belongings taken by the barons. At the same time many crimes went unpunished.

Henry decided to do something about this. He set up his own courts. Most people used them because they were fairer than the barons' courts. Money from fines in the new courts went to the king. Henry needed this money – especially to pay for wars against unruly barons. Raising money from fines was much more popular with the people than paying taxes.

Activities

1. Describe what is happening in Source A.
2. Which of the following explanations for Henry setting up his own courts is supported by Source B?
   - He wanted to raise money from fines.
   - He wanted to reduce the amount of crime.
   - He wanted to take power from the barons.
   - He wanted to see that everyone was treated fairly.
   - He wanted to protect the poor and the weak.

   Explain your answer.
3. Using all the information in this chapter work in pairs to construct an interview with Henry II in 1154. The interviewer should point out the problems the king faces and Henry should explain how he intends to overcome them.

Checklist

- Henry II ruled a large empire. This was a difficult task.
- Henry ordered castles to be pulled down and made the barons obey him.
- Henry travelled around his lands with his household constantly checking on what was going on for himself.
- Law and order were important to Henry. He set up his own courts and chose judges whom he could trust to be fair.

Source A

A law court like those set up by Henry II

Source B

King Henry believed it was his duty to prevent his subjects from running about the country robbing the poor, harming widows and orphans, raping virgins and especially from shedding blood. Those who illegally hunted wild animals would be punished with a heavy fine or long imprisonment. Murder was to be punished by hanging, traitors were to be sent into exile in another country, those caught for less serious crimes would have their hands cut off. The king was very concerned to show fair treatment to everyone so he chose people he could trust as judges.

'Chronicles of Ralph of Diceto', late 12th century

8 KING AND BARONS

1199	John crowned king.
1204	John loses control of Normandy.
1208	English churches closed.
1209	John expelled from the church.
1214	Battle of Bouvines.
1215	Magna Carta and civil war.
1216	John dies. Henry III crowned king.

Henry III

1258	Henry III forced to accept Magna Carta.
1263	Simon de Montfort rebels and seizes control of government.
1265	Simon de Montfort killed at the Battle of Evesham.
1272	Henry III dies. Edward I crowned king.

Edward II

1307	Edward I dies. Edward II crowned king.
1321	Civil war.
1326	Civil war. Edward II captured.
1327	Edward II murdered.

Themes

Henry II was a successful king. The barons obeyed him and paid the taxes he demanded. Other kings were not so successful. For example, John, Henry III and Edward II all found that at times their barons and bishops refused to obey them.

These kings were very unpopular with many of their subjects. In each case the barons became so angry with the way the king behaved that they rebelled against him.

This chapter asks the following questions.

- Why were these kings so unpopular?
- What action did the barons and bishops take against them?

In 1215 King John met the barons and bishops at Runnymede. The Focus looks at what happened as Stephen Langton, the Archbishop of Canterbury, might have seen it.

Focus Activities

Read the passage opposite.

1. What was Magna Carta?
2. How did the barons and bishops get John to agree to Magna Carta? Explain your answer fully.
3. Write an account of the meeting from King John's point of view.

Diary of Stephen Langton, Archbishop of Canterbury

What a month! I hope and pray that today I helped prevent war and bloodshed and brought peace to our land.

This morning we met King John at Runnymede, an island in the River Thames near Windsor Castle. It was a bright, sunny day. John sat at a table in a field filled with brightly coloured tents. He did not look happy.

For over six months John has refused to accept the demands of his barons and bishops. But our capture of London a few weeks ago seems to have convinced him that he has no other choice. He knows that the alternative is war.

We have drawn up a document known as Magna Carta – The Great Charter. It contains 63 demands. John has wronged so many people – including myself. He can't go on like this. If he agrees to Magna Carta it should stop him from doing just as he pleases.

The air was filled with tension and excitement. I walked over and handed Magna Carta to King John. He put his seal to the document. At last he has agreed to our demands.

So – it is done! But I do not trust the king. He has gone back on his promises before. What more can be done, though? I have a suspicion that the king is only playing for time. When this crisis is over and things calm down, will he raise an army and try to punish us? I pray he does not, but he is a very cunning man.

King John

Unpopular kings

This section looks at why John, Henry III and Edward II were so unpopular. In the reign of each, the powerful men of the kingdom – the barons and bishops – were unhappy with the way the king ruled.

Many of their complaints were about the king:

- losing wars
- demanding high taxes
- choosing favourites as advisers
- ill-treating his people.

These complaints were described in chronicles, written by monks.

Activities

1. Using the information in this section:
   a) Copy and complete the table below. In each column put a tick if the complaint was made about that king and a cross if it was not.

Complaint	John	Henry III	Edward II
Losing wars			
Demanding high taxes			
Choosing favourites as advisers			
Ill-treating people/ causing suffering			
Treatment of the church			

   b) Which *two* types of complaint were made most often?
   c) Who do you think was the most unpopular king? Give reasons for your answer.

2. Should we believe everything monks wrote in chronicles, especially about King John? Explain your answer.

Source A   King John, 1199-1216

Complaint 1: He lost wars in France.
John fought wars against the French king. During these wars the French captured land in France which, at that time, belonged to the English. John was unable to win this land back and was finally defeated at the Battle of Bouvines in 1214.

Complaint 2: He demanded high taxes.
John ordered the barons either to provide knights (soldiers) for the army in France or to pay a tax instead. The barons refused. They did not see why they should have to pay for John's mistakes in France.

Complaint 3: He ill-treated people.
Chroniclers claimed that John's officials put men in prison without trial and put others to death and that he allowed the families of barons to be tortured and priests to be beaten up.

Complaint 4: He argued with the church.
John argued with the pope over who should be Archbishop of Canterbury. The pope had usually chosen bishops and archbishops. Now John wanted to choose them himself. The pope ordered all churches in England to be closed as a punishment. He also expelled John from the church – this was called excommunication and was a very serious punishment.

Source B   King Henry III, 1216-1272

Complaint 1: He lost wars in France.
Henry took an army to France three times to try to win back the land his father, John, had lost. Each time he failed.

Complaint 2: He wasted money and demanded high taxes.
In 1258 Henry tried to have his second son, Edmund, crowned King of Sicily. Large sums of money were sent to the pope, who controlled Sicily and decided who would be king there. The attempt failed.

Complaint 3: He chose his favourites as advisers.
Henry ignored the advice of his English barons. Instead he preferred the advice of the friends and relatives of his French wife. He gave them important jobs. The English barons were very angry.

Complaint 4: He treated people unfairly.
Henry was mean. For example, the people of London gave him a gift of a hundred pounds. But because he regularly received gifts from them, he had come to expect it. He was heard commenting, 'I am not saying thank you to the people of London for paying me what they owe'.

Source C   King Edward II, 1307-1327

Complaint 1: He lost the war with Scotland.
In 1314 the English were defeated by the Scottish army at the Battle of Bannockburn. People said Edward was a coward because he ran away from the battlefield.

Complaint 2: He caused people to suffer.
During 1315 and 1316 there were many storms in England. The harvest was ruined and people starved. Many people said it was the king's fault. God was punishing the people for his bad behaviour.

Complaint 3: He chose his favourites as advisers.
Edward chose first Piers Gaveston and then Hugh le Despenser as advisers. He took their advice, whether it was good or bad, on everything and rewarded them with lands and wealth. Gaveston treated the other barons as if he was a second king. These favourites were hated by everyone.

Complaint 4: He treated his wife badly.
Edward often insulted his wife, Isabella, in public. In the end she led a rebellion against him.

Magna Carta

The Focus passage described how the barons and bishops tried to control the way King John behaved. Source A gives some of the demands from Magna Carta – the agreement they made with him.

However, Magna Carta did not solve the problems. John broke the agreement almost immediately and there was a civil war between the king and his nobles. John died in 1216. The new king, Henry III, was only nine years old when he came to the throne. In 1225 he agreed to obey Magna Carta by putting his seal to it (Source B).

Source B   A copy of Magna Carta

Henry III's seal on a copy of Magna Carta dated 1225

Source C   Henry III and Magna Carta

At Oxford (in 1258), the barons still insisted that the king (Henry III) obey Magna Carta, which his father, John, had agreed to (and which Henry had ignored). The barons also demanded that officials be chosen to put right what the king had done wrong.

Matthew Paris, 1258

Source A   Some demands from Magna Carta

1. The English church shall be free (especially to choose its own bishops and have its own courts).
2. No tax is to be collected by the king unless it is agreed to by the archbishops, bishops, abbots and barons.
3. No knight shall be forced to do more service in the army than he owes.
4. No official of the king shall use his own evidence to find a man guilty. He must have reliable witnesses to support him.
5. No one shall be put in prison unless he is found guilty of breaking the law by his equals (a jury).
6. Only men who know the laws of the kingdom and obey them will be given jobs as judges and officials.

Magna Carta, 1215

Activities

1. Study Source A. Using the information on King John (page 46), work out why each of these demands was included in Magna Carta. Give your answers in a table like this:

Demand	Why it was included in Magna Carta
1 2 3	

2. By putting his seal to Magna Carta in 1225 Henry III agreed to its demands. Did he keep this agreement? Use Source C and information from page 47 to help you with your answer.

3. a) Which of the clauses of Magna Carta listed in Source A are still in force today?

    b) Do you think they are important? Give reasons for your answer.

Civil wars

What happened when a king took no notice of the barons' demands or broke his agreements with them? If the barons felt strongly enough they might rebel against the king.

In just over 100 years there were four civil wars in England. The barons fought John in 1215, Henry III in 1263 and Edward II in 1321 and 1326.

In 1326 Edward II found that most important people in his kingdom, including his wife Isabella, were against him. Facing defeat he agreed to hand over the crown to his son. His favourite, Hugh le Despenser, was captured, tortured and executed. Edward was imprisoned in Berkeley Castle and later murdered – in such a way, the story goes, that his screams could be heard two miles away, but there was not a mark on his body.

Source A   The end of Edward II's reign

Civil war, which was nothing new to the English, was started by Queen Isabella's armed force. The king had learned from his advisers that most of his barons and almost all his kingdom were supporting his wife. He set off for Wales. The king and Hugh le Despenser were captured.

The Bishop of Hereford said that it was the king's duty to hand over his crown to his son, for if he refused, they would choose another to be king who knew better how to rule his kingdom.

'Chronicle of Geoffrey le Baker', 1326 and 1327

Source B   Hugh le Despenser's execution

Nobles were normally allowed the swiftest form of execution – beheading. On this occasion things were rather different. First, Despenser was crowned with nettles. Then he was placed on a high gallows. There, parts of his body were cut off and burnt in front of him. His crimes were then read out as he was hanged, drawn and quartered.

Activities

1. Read Source A.
   a) What action did the barons and bishops take against Edward II?
   b) Why do you think they took this action? (See Source C, page 47)
   c) Edward II agreed to hand over the crown to his son. Why do you think he did this?
2. Using Source B, write a newspaper report describing the execution of Hugh le Despenser. Explain to your readers why he was executed in this way. (See Source C, page 47)
3. Choose one of the kings in this chapter. Make up a conversation between the king and one of his barons giving the king's point of view.

Checklist

- Some kings were very unpopular with their barons.
- The barons made agreements to try and control the behaviour of these kings.
- Magna Carta was the most important of these agreements.
- The barons were prepared to fight civil wars and even replace the king if they felt it was necessary.

9 PARLIAMENT

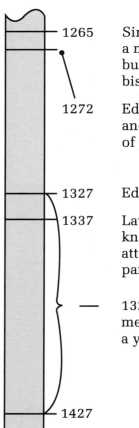

1265	Simon de Montfort calls a meeting of knights, burgesses, barons and bishops.
1272	Edward I becomes king and calls regular meetings of parliament.
1327	Edward III becomes king.
1337	Law passed which says that knights and burgesses must attend meetings of parliament.
	1327-1427 Parliament meets on average once a year.
1427	

Parliament usually met in the king's palace at Westminster where the modern Houses of Parliament now stand.

Themes

Most medieval kings were strong leaders who made their own decisions and expected people to obey them. However, kings often discussed such things as taxes with the barons and bishops in meetings known as Great Councils. The king's most important subjects were more likely to agree if they were consulted first, rather than just ordered to pay.

By the end of the 13th century knights from the counties and burgesses from the towns also came to meetings with the king. These meetings were now known as parliaments. This name came from the French word *parler*, which means 'to talk'. At meetings of parliament the king announced his plans and asked for new taxes. Those who attended found that this was a good time to ask the king to listen to their complaints.

This chapter asks the following questions.

- How and why did parliament develop?
- What part did it play in government?

We start by looking at the first meeting of barons, bishops, knights and burgesses. It was called by Simon de Montfort in 1265. There had been a civil war between Henry III and his barons and in 1265 England was ruled by the barons' leader, Simon de Montfort. The Focus is a diary entry he might have written in January 1265.

Focus Activities

Read the passage opposite.
1. Why did Simon de Montfort invite knights and burgesses as well as barons and bishops to meet with him?
2. Divide into pairs. One take the part of a knight or burgess who supports Simon de Montfort, the other a baron who opposes him. You both come to the meeting held in 1265. What will you say to each other about the situation?

A kingdom without a king

Well, I think I've reached crisis point. Since I defeated Henry III's forces and took him and his son, Prince Edward, prisoner at the Battle of Lewes last year, things have not been easy.

Although I had lots of support at first, things seem to have changed. Many of the barons are now saying that I'm behaving like a king myself. Perhaps they've already forgotten how the king treated them – how he gave their land and money to all those foreigners he brought in. Well, what do they expect me to do? I won't treat them like Henry did, but I do have to decide what is best for the country and they have to obey me. We've always had kings – how else can I run the country? I'm worried that some of the barons will turn completely against me.

To make matters worse, Prince Edward has escaped from prison. This really is bad news. He's a good fighter and people respect him – much more than his father. I must do something to get myself more support.

I have decided what to do. I shall call a special meeting – a bit like the Great Council. I can't expect all the barons and bishops to support me so I'll ask each county to send two knights and each town two burgesses. After all they are important people – they have much land and wealth between them and they too suffered under King Henry's rule. They'll probably support me against the barons. The knights, being small landowners, will enjoy feeling equal to their overlords. And many of the burgesses in the towns are no friends of the barons – they remember having to do work service for their overlords before they bought their charters. All being well, the invitation to this meeting will make them feel important and they'll want to help me run the country.

With any luck I'll be able to get enough support to rule on my own and defeat Prince Edward.

Simon de Montfort did not rule England for long. He was defeated and killed by Prince Edward at the Battle of Evesham in August 1265. This picture shows his body being carried away.

The origins of Parliament

Although he might not have realised it, Simon de Montfort had brought about an important change. When Edward I came to the throne in 1272 he also called parliaments which included knights and burgesses as well as barons and bishops.

Between April and July 1290 Edward met his barons and bishops to discuss his plans. The knights and burgesses were only asked to attend for the last week of the meeting when taxes were being discussed.

Edward called parliaments to get more money. People had become more prosperous over the last century – especially the burgesses – and Edward wanted a share of their wealth. Source B shows that he got much more of his money from taxes than kings had done in the past. People were more likely to agree to new taxes if they were able to discuss them with the king in parliament – especially if he also listened to their complaints.

Source A   A Great Council

The king meets his barons and bishops. Knights and burgesses did not attend.

Source B   Where the king's money came from

	Year	
	1130	1272
From his own lands and feudal dues	87%	43%
From taxes	13%	57%

Source C   Edward I's parliament

Edward meets his barons and bishops. Burgesses and knights also attended but had to use a separate room. (This sixteenth century picture wrongly includes the rulers of Scotland and Wales.)

Activities

1. Look at Sources A and C. What are the similarities and differences between Edward I's parliament and the Great Council?

2. Study the percentages in Source B.
   a) Where did the king get most of his money (i) in 1130 (ii) in 1272?
   b) How might this change help explain why parliament replaced the Great Council towards the end of the thirteenth century?

3. Why do you think the ordinary villagers did not have a say in what happened in parliament?

The role of Parliament

By the time of Edward I's death parliament played an important part in the way the king governed the country. It helped him pass laws as well as agreeing to taxation. It had even begun to help the king punish barons who had disobeyed him. In 1337 Edward agreed that whenever the lords – that is, the barons and bishops – met, the commoners, or commons, as the knights and burgesses became known, should come as well. They met in a separate room, which is how we get the names House of Lords and House of Commons, which are still in use today.

The king stayed firmly in control and only called parliament when he needed it – perhaps once a year – but he knew how useful it was. He needed it to agree to taxes. In return, he listened to complaints from parliament. The king was usually happy to agree to requests, like the one made in Source B, in return for taxes.

Source A   Agreeing to taxes

Parliament gathered together and the king asked the members for a tax to pay for the war. At first they refused, but after a few days the barons agreed to give an eleventh part of their goods; the boroughs gave up a seventh part. Eventually the churchmen agreed to give up a tenth part of their goods.

Bartholomew Cotton, 'History of England', 1295

Source B   A request from parliament

Edward, the king's father, took all that belonged to the bishops. As a result there has been great damage, waste and destruction to their possessions, parks and woods. Because of this the people ask that the bishops be repaid for all the damage.

'Petition from parliament', 1327

Source D   Parliament as a law court

To our lord the king from parliament. John Maltravers can prove that he was wrongly banished (sent away) from the kingdom of England. And may it please our lord the king to allow John to come back to England.

'Petition from parliament', 1339

Source C   Agreeing to laws

1487. Taking the Lord Chancellor's advice parliament agreed to several excellent laws to carry out what the king wished.

Francis Bacon, 'History of Henry VII', 1621

Activities

1. Look at Source A.
   a) Why do you think the king did not find it easy to get parliament to agree to a new tax? Explain your answer.
   b) What do you think a king might have done to persuade parliament to agree to new taxes?

2. Study Sources A–D. What were the advantages of having a parliament
   a) to the king
   b) to the barons, bishops, knights and burgesses?

Checklist

- Early medieval kings sometimes discussed their decisions with the barons and bishops.
- Simon de Montfort asked knights and burgesses as well as barons and bishops to come to a meeting with him.
- Edward I summoned both barons and bishops and knights and burgesses to attend meetings when he wanted new taxes – these meetings became known as parliaments.
- During the fourteenth century parliament played a more important part in government, though it only met when the king wanted.

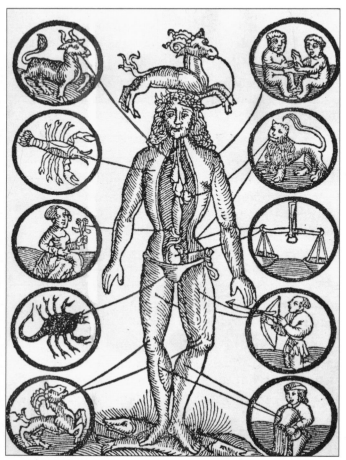

In the Middle Ages doctors used the positions of stars and planets to decide what was wrong with a patient.

Clothes of people who died from the Black Death being burnt

Themes

In the summer of 1348 England became a land of fear. A mysterious disease known as the Black Death swept the country. No one knew who would be struck down next. Coughs and sneezes gave way to large lumps which came up in the armpit or in the groin. Dark blotches appeared on the body. This was followed by fever and vomiting – the victims often becoming delirious and coughing up blood before they died, racked with pain.

Doctors were helpless in the face of the Black Death. There were few of them and they did not know what caused the disease nor how to cure it.

This chapter asks the following questions about health and disease in the Middle Ages.

- How healthy were people?
- What was the Black Death and how did it spread?
- How did people explain disease?
- How did they treat it?

We start by looking at a village struck by the Black Death in 1348. This diary is based on actual historical evidence.

Focus Activities

Read the passage opposite.

1. What does the writer think has caused the Black Death?

2. Why do you think people found the disease so frightening? Give as many reasons as you can.

3. You are to speak at Father John's funeral. Write a short speech about his work in the village during the past week.

Diary of the Black Death, 1348

Monday: Father John reports that a dreadful sickness has struck the village. Yesterday everyone attended Matins, the morning service, but members of five families were missing at Vespers in the evening. Relatives say that they have the sweating sickness and fever. May God preserve us! I pray that this is not the Black Death which has visited so many villages in this area.

Tuesday: Ten more families are affected. Seven people died yesterday. Father John is mixing up honey, vinegar and herbs to put on the black lumps that appear on the victims' bodies. It will do no harm, but I doubt it will do good either. Nothing seems to work against this terrible disease.

Wednesday: People are dying hourly. We cannot dig graves fast enough and so must make do with one large pit for all. No one knows where it will strike next. Everyone is frightened and the church is full with people praying for their loved ones.

Thursday: Why us, O Lord? Have we really been so evil that we deserve such a terrible punishment? Where does it come from, this Black Death? Will no one be left alive? Even the children are taken from us and mothers watch them die before they, too, are struck down.

Friday: Father John is dead. God rest his soul! He was visiting the sick when he suddenly collapsed. The black swellings came upon him and in a few hours he could recognise no one. By dusk he was dead. Will it never end?

Saturday: The village is quiet now apart from the sound of a gentle wind blowing through the trees. Only a few people are left. Dogs sit faithfully by the doors of houses that are empty and silent. Cattle and oxen wander around the fields with no one to look after them. Who will harvest the barley that was sown in the spring? Who will plough the land for next year's crops?

So many people died from the Black Death that they had to be buried in mass graves.

Life and death

Today less than one in a hundred babies die in their first year of life. In the Middle Ages about a quarter died before they were one year old. Infections of the ear or chest, which nowadays are quickly cured with antibiotics, often caused death. Diseases like leprosy, smallpox and influenza were very common.

For those lucky enough to survive childhood, a poor diet, unhygienic living conditions, illness and accidents often led to an early death. There were no antiseptics (such as 'Dettol' or 'TCP') to prevent infection in cuts and wounds. So the treatment of a serious leg wound, for example, was to have the leg cut off. Otherwise a bad infection like gangrene could easily set in.

Despite this gloomy picture, most adults seem to have been quite healthy, though they did not live as long as we expect to. The rich, who did not work so hard and ate better food than the people who worked for them, were likely to live longer.

Source B Length of a peasant's life

In the early fourteenth century peasants who survived childhood in Halesowen expected to live into their mid-forties.

Conclusions from a study of the 'Halesowen Court Rolls', 1980

Source C A cripple

Some people, though otherwise fit, had deformities caused by problems before or during birth.

Source A Norton Priory skeletons

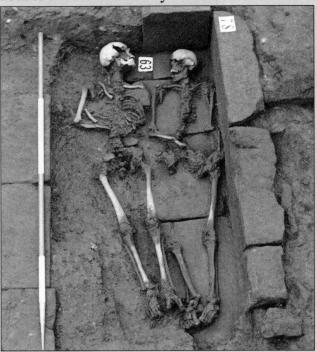

Archaeologists can learn a lot about medieval people's health from skeletons. These skeletons of wealthy people were discovered at Norton Priory in Cheshire. They were only slightly smaller than people today and some lived into their 50s and 60s. Their teeth were in much better condition, probably because they ate very little sugar. Arthritis (a disease affecting the joints) was common, especially of the spine.

Norton Priory Museum Trust, 1991

Activities

1. What does the information on this page tell us about the health of medieval people?

2. How might you explain the different conclusions reached by the writers of Sources A and B about the length of people's lives in the Middle Ages?

Writing in 1260, Master Alderotti, a doctor, suggested that washing each morning was one way to stay healthy. His advice was difficult to follow. There were no taps to provide clean water for washing or drinking. It had to be fetched from a stream, river or well.

There was no organised collection of rubbish in medieval towns and villages. There were no drains, proper toilets or pipes to carry away dirty water and sewage. Rubbish and waste piled up in the streets and, helped by the rain, soaked into the ground, often finding its way into water supplies.

We know today that germs breed in dirt and rubbish and cause disease. Medieval people knew nothing of germs – they had no microscopes through which they could have seen them. Some people, though, did begin to make the connection between rubbish and disease, believing that unpleasant smells might be the cause of infection.

Source G   Dirty towns

The king has found out that the city streets are so full of rubbish from the houses that the air is infected and the city is poisoned. This is dangerous to everyone.

Letter written by Edward III, 1349

Source D   Dirty people

Thomas Becket wore a shirt which reached to his knees and swarmed with lice.

William FitzStephen, c.1170

Source E   Dirty houses

The floors are usually made of clay covered with straw. Under the straw is a mixture of beer, grease, bones, animal droppings and everything that is nasty.

Erasmus, c.1515

Source F   Public toilets

The only public toilets in London were on London Bridge. They emptied straight into the River Thames.

3. a) Study Sources D-G. Copy the table below and fill in the details for each source.

Source	Threats to health mentioned	How they are dealt with nowadays
D		
E		
F		
G		

b) How might this information help explain why people's lives were so short?

c) Is there any evidence in Sources D-G to show that people thought that dirt might cause disease? Explain your answer.

The Black Death

The Black Death was the name medieval people gave to the plague. The most common type was bubonic plague. The main symptoms were fever and swelling (buboes) in the armpits and in the groin. Historians think that about one person in every three died of the plague between 1348 and 1351.

In the fourteenth century no one understood what caused the disease or how it was spread. We now know that it was spread by fleas and black rats. When a flea from an infected rat bit a human being it passed the disease into the person's bloodstream. Many people had fleas. Rats could always be found in the rubbish that filled the streets of towns and villages. Other types of plague could be passed through the air, on the breath, and even by touch.

The Black Death came to England through trade. It travelled from China and India through the Middle East to Europe, following the great trade routes. Ships carried infected people and infected rats. Both landed at ports across Europe.

Source A

Fleas from infected rats passed the disease on to human beings.

Source B   Plague reaches England (1)

It began in India. Then the dreadful disease reached England. It started at Southampton and spread along the coast. It reached Bristol where almost everyone in the town died.

'Chronicle of Henry Knighton', 1349

Source D   Plague reaches England (2)

In this year, at Melcombe in the county of Dorset, a little before the feast of St John the Baptist (24th June), two ships, one of them from Bristol, came into harbour. One of the sailors had brought with him, from Gascony in France, the disease and through him the people of Melcombe were the first in England to be infected.

'Grey Friar's Chronicle', 1348

Source C   The spread of the disease

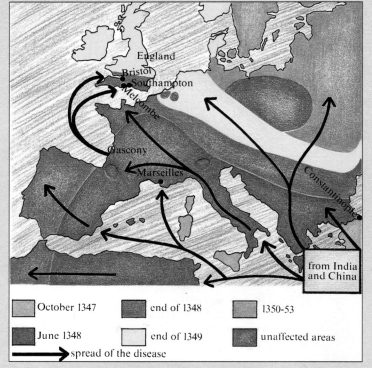

▨ October 1347		▨ end of 1348		▨ 1350-53	
▨ June 1348		▨ end of 1349		▨ unaffected areas	
→ spread of the disease					

Medieval people had little idea about what really caused the plague. It was suggested that being stared at by an infected person could cause the plague, or even sex with an older woman. Some thought it was caused by poisonous snakes and lizards dropping out of the sky.

Advice on how to avoid or cure the plague was even stranger, ranging from shutting oneself up alone and fasting, to carrying posies of herbs and flowers, or even cutting a live pigeon in half and applying it to the swellings!

Many people saw the plague as a punishment from God for their sins. To prove they were sorry and so escape the disease some became 'flagellants'. They wandered the country praying, beating themselves with sharp-ended whips and preaching their message to all who would listen.

Source E   Flagellants

Source F   Causes of the plague

Fire fell down like rain. It destroyed all the land and killed the people. Then there were huge amounts of smoke – anyone looking at this died in less than twelve hours. Also, anyone who looked at someone who had seen the smoke quickly died.

'Chronicler of Este', c.1346

Source G   A cure for the plague

Toads should be thoroughly dried in the sun. They should be laid on the boil. The toad will swell and draw out the poison of the plague to its own body. When it is full it should be thrown away and a new one applied.

Guy de Chauliac, c.1348

Activities

1. Use Sources B and C to explain how the plague came to England.

2. a) In what way do the writers of Sources B and D disagree about how the plague came to England?

   b) What might explain this difference?

3. Look at Source A. From what you learned in the last section about hygiene in towns and villages (pages 56-7), give reasons why the plague spread so quickly.

4. Study Source F.

   a) Were fire and smoke really the cause of the plague? Explain your answer.

   b) Why do you think this writer thought they were the cause?

5. Why do you think medieval people might try cures for the plague like the one described in Source G?

6. Some flagellants (Source E) have arrived in your village. An argument takes place between two villagers. One wants to join them, the other does not. What might they say to each other?

7. If medieval doctors had modern knowledge about the plague, what laws might have been passed to stop it spreading?

Medicine in the Middle Ages

In the Middle Ages people had little understanding of the causes or treatment of disease. Doctors believed that the body contained four substances called 'humours' – blood, phlegm, yellow bile and black bile. When these humours became unbalanced a person suffered ill-health. It was the doctor's task to put the balance right. Too little of a humour meant it must be topped up, too much meant some must be let out.

A doctor trained for many years and studied books in Greek and Latin. Diagnosis – identifying the disease – was made through astrology, taking the pulse or studying the way a bird reacted to the patient. Treatments included pills, ointments, bloodletting and enemas.

Surgeons were often barbers and were not as well respected as doctors. Poor people could afford neither and put their faith in the local priest, or the wise woman with her knowledge of herbs and plants.

Source C   A doctor (2)

Modern doctors possess three special qualifications and these are: to be able to lie without being caught out; to pretend to be honest; and to cause death without feeling guilty.

Written in 1380

Source D   Treating illness

To stop the humours overflowing several kinds of medicine may work, such as special diet, drinks or a hot bath. Vomiting and letting out blood will also help.

Salerno Medical School, 11th century

Source A   A doctor (1)

The doctor must know how to read so that he can understand medical books. He must know how to write and speak well so that he can explain the diseases he is treating. He must have a good mind to investigate and cure the causes of disease. Arithmetic is also important, so that he can count the hours a person is in pain. Music will also be useful, for it can be a great help to the sick. Lastly he must know astronomy so that he can study the stars and seasons, because our bodies change with the planets and stars.

Isidore, c.620

Source B

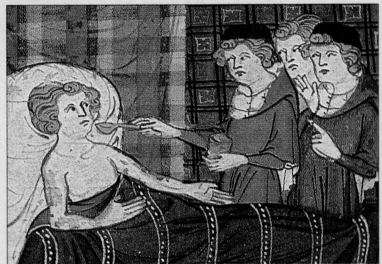

A patient is given some medicine to restore the balance of humours in his body.

Activities

1. a) Using Source A, make a list of the skills required by a doctor in the Middle Ages. Place them in the order you think they would be useful for curing disease.

    b) Do you think a modern doctor needs the same skills? Explain your answer.

    c) Do you think the 'qualifications' mentioned in Source C would be useful to medieval doctors? Explain your answer.

2. Do you think the treatments in Sources B and D would be likely to work? Explain your answer.

Having an operation in the Middle Ages was a very risky business. There were no anaesthetics to put patients to sleep and they sometimes died of shock. Wounds often became infected because of lack of cleanliness. There were no antiseptics to prevent infection.

Source F   Removing a leg

The surgeon turned to the knight and said, 'Which would you prefer – to live with one leg or to die with two?' When the knight replied that he would prefer to live with one leg, the surgeon sent for a strong man and a sharp axe. He put the knight's leg on the block of wood and said, 'Strike a mighty blow and cut cleanly'. The man struck the knight one blow and then another. The patient died at once.

'The Biography of Usama', 12th century

Checklist

- Although most adults were quite healthy, medieval people did not live as long as we do.

- Infectious diseases were common, killing in particular the young and old.

- In 1348 a plague struck. It came to England along trade routes from the East.

- The plague was carried by fleas on rats. It spread quickly. About one third of the people in England died from it.

- Doctors knew little about the causes of diseases and were not very successful at curing them.

Source E   A nose operation

Source G   A modern operating theatre

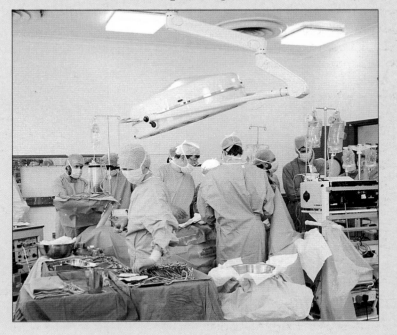

3. Read Source F. Why do you think the knight died?
4. What are the main differences between the operations in Sources E and F and those carried out today – Source G?

11 THE GREAT REVOLT

12th June	60,000 rebels camp at Blackheath and Mile End on either side of the River Thames.
13th June	City gates opened. Buildings burned, prisons broken open and people murdered.
14th June	The king meets Wat Tyler, one of the rebel leaders, at Mile End. The king agrees to end work service. Many people go home after this meeting. That night the rebels break into the Tower of London and murder the Archbishop of Canterbury.
15th June	The king meets Wat Tyler at Smithfield. The king agrees that land belonging to the lords and church should be divided up among the people. Wat Tyler is killed and the king leads the rebels out of the city.

Themes

In 1381 a huge army arrived in London. It pulled down houses and set them on fire. It murdered the Archbishop of Canterbury and other important men. Was this some foreign invader come to conquer England? No, this army was made up of the people of England – villagers, traders, craftsmen and even priests.

The rebels had a list of demands – higher wages and lower taxes and an end to work service. They marched on London from all parts of the country. Most came from Essex and Kent where angry crowds had driven out tax collectors who demanded payment of the third poll tax in five years.

This chapter looks at the rebellion which is known as the Great Revolt. It asks the following questions.

- What were the causes of the revolt?
- Why did it take place in 1381?
- What did the rebels want?
- What happened after the revolt?

The Focus looks at a meeting between the king and the rebels at Smithfield on 15th June 1381. This is how the story might appear in a newspaper today.

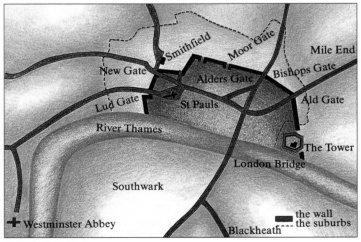

London, 1381

Focus Activities

The Focus is based on the writings of churchmen and nobles. They supported the king. Their dislike of the rebels, and Wat Tyler in particular, comes across clearly.

Write an account of the meeting at Smithfield from the rebels' point of view. Think how the 'facts' could be described and explained in a different way.

Crisis at Smithfield

London was saved yesterday by the quick thinking of our noble young king, Richard II.

As he had promised, the king went with a group of advisers to meet the rebels at Smithfield. This followed the meeting at Mile End at which King Richard promised the rebels freedom from their lords and an end to work service.

In the dusty heat of the dying day the rebel leader, Wat Tyler, rode up to the king on a small pony. Dismounting, he half bowed, then dared to shake the king by the hand, not even taking off his cap! The king took no offence at this and asked Tyler what the rebels wanted. Tyler replied that as well as the charters of freedom that were being written for them, they wanted the king's word that land would be taken from the lords and the church and divided among the people. He threatened that the lords of England would regret it if these things were not settled.

The king tried to calm Tyler down and said he would agree to his demands. But the rebel leader continued to act rudely and called for a flask of water to rinse his mouth. He spat it out in a disgusting fashion, typical of an ignorant peasant, and then demanded ale which he drank down in huge gulps.

This is two pictures in one. On the left King Richard watches the murder of Wat Tyler. On the right he tells the rebels that he is their leader.

A quarrel broke out between Tyler and a squire – one of the king's men. The squire shouted that Tyler was the greatest thief and robber in Kent. The rebel leader lashed out at him with a dagger. The Mayor tried to stop the fight and would have been badly wounded by Tyler had he not been wearing armour. In the scuffle which followed, Tyler was dragged from his horse and stabbed to death. Seeing their leader fall, the rebels drew their bows with shouts of 'Kill them all!'

Bravely the king rode out in front of them. 'Gentlemen', he said, 'What do you want? I am your leader. Follow me!' With this, he led the mob out of the city to Clerkenwell Field.

Thanks to the actions of our young king, the revolt appears to be over. Pardons have been granted to all the rebels, who are returning to their homes with all haste.

However, such a wicked uprising by people who do not know their place can surely not go unpunished!

The effects of the Black Death

The peasants and their leaders were angry enough to leave their homes and march – some more than 100 miles – to London. This was a big step for them to take. Why did they do it? A peasant's life was hard – but it always had been, and there had been no revolt of this size before.

The Black Death had killed perhaps a third of England's population. This meant that life could no longer go on in the same way. There were not enough people to plough the fields and harvest the crops. Peasants could not cope with their own work let alone do work service for their lord.

With fewer tenants the lords wanted more work rather than less. But their tenants wanted to end work service so they could rent land and work for whoever paid them most. In some parts of the country work service had ended long before the plague. Tenants had become labourers who worked for wages. After the Black Death they demanded higher wages from the lords.

Source A

Sheep and oxen wandered free through the fields and among the crops, and there was no one to drive them off. When harvest time came higher wages were not enough to get people to gather in the crops which rotted in the fields.

'Chronicle of Henry Knighton', 1348-49

Source B

At Woodeaton there were only two farmers left and they would have gone away if the abbot had not made a new agreement with them to reduce their work service. At the deserted village of Wyville in Lincolnshire the land is worth little because it is poor and stony. It is not being used as there are no people left to farm it after the plague.

Records of Eynsham Abbey, c.1385

Source C

The remains of a deserted village in Leicestershire – the people who lived there all died of the plague.

Source D   A new law

The king sent an order to all the counties that labourers should not be paid more than before the plague. But the labourers were so proud and stubborn that they would not listen to the king's command. If anyone wanted to employ them he had to pay them what they wanted or lose his fruit and crops. Then the king ordered many labourers to be arrested and put in prison.

'Chronicle of Henry Knighton', 1351

Source E

You could hardly get a priest to look after a church for less than £10 a year. There had been plenty of priests before the plague. Then you could get a priest for £2 and his food. But at this time very few would take the job at £20 a year.

'Chronicle of Henry Knighton', 1349

Source F

It is sad but the whole world was changed for the worse. People were meaner and more greedy than before, even though they had more things. They were jealous of each other and there was an increase in the number of fights, arguments and law cases.

Jean de Venette, 1349

Source G

As soon as masters accuse their workers of bad work or try to pay them less they leave and quickly find jobs in new places at higher wages. Masters dare not upset their workers and so have to give them whatever they ask for.

Introduction to a law, 1376

Activities

1. a) Copy the table below showing the effects of the Black Death. Against each source tick the effects which are mentioned.

Source	Some villages were deserted and fell into ruins.	There were not enough people to do the work.	People wanted more money for their work.	People became mean and greedy.
A				
B				
C				
D				
E				
F				
G				

b) Why do you think people could ask for higher wages and get them?

c) Do you think Jean de Venette (Source F) gives a true picture? Give reasons for your answer.

2. You have been asked by the king to write a report on the effects of the Black Death. Write your report using the evidence in Sources A-G.

3. Look at Sources D and G.
   a) According to Source D what did the king do to try to keep wages down?
   b) Why do you think he did this?
   c) Did it work? Explain your answer.

What did the rebels want?

The poll tax of 1380 sparked off the Great Revolt. The money was needed for the war with France. Poll taxes were very unpopular and this was the third in five years. It was more than a week's wages for most people.

In 1381 Richard II was only fourteen years old and so important nobles governed England. They were blamed for the poll tax. People refused to pay it and attacked the tax collectors – the revolt had begun.

Lords' manor houses were attacked and records of work service destroyed. It was not just the peasants that rose up against their lords – there were merchants and traders, churchmen and craftsmen, freemen as well as villeins. People wanted freedom – from the feudal system, from work service and from the lord's control of the towns.

Source A The poll tax

Parliament granted the king a tax of two shillings from each married man. The unmarried paid one shilling. Yet this tax did not bring in as large a sum as the tax of 4 pence in the previous year.

'Chronicle of Henry Knighton', 1381

Source B

Richard II with the noblemen who ruled England

Source C Peasant anger

The people of Fobbing, Corringham and Stanford-le-Hope numbered over a hundred. They went to Thomas de Bampton – the tax collector – and told him they would not give him any money. At this, Thomas ordered his men to arrest the villagers and put them in prison. But the villagers attacked Thomas and his men and it looked as if they were going to kill them. Thomas then fled to London.

'Anonimalle Chronicle', 1381

Activities

1. Why do you think the poll tax of 1380 brought in less money than the poll tax of 1379?

2. Study Source C. What evidence is there that people were angry about the poll tax?

3. Look at Source B. Why do you think noblemen were blamed for the poll tax?

4. Using information on this page design a poster telling people why they should not pay the poll tax of 1380.

One of the leaders of the revolt was a priest called John Ball. For several years he had been travelling around Kent stirring people up to rebel against their lords. Crowds gathered in towns and villages to listen to his sermons.

Source E

We have no one we can complain to or who is willing to listen to us. Let us go to the king and argue with him. He is young and may help. If not we must put things right ourselves.

John Ball, 1381

Source F   John Ball

The rebels had been stirred up and encouraged in their lunatic ideas by a mad priest called John Ball. He had often been in prison for what he preached in the villages after mass on Sundays. John Ball's ideas were well known to many of the ordinary people of London who were jealous of wealthy noblemen. They were saying that England was being robbed of its silver and gold by those who called themselves noble.

Jean Froissart, c.1381

Source D

The villeins went to the church of St Mary to discuss their services to the monastery. They wanted land around the town where they could graze their animals freely. They wanted to fish, hunt deer, pheasants and ducks without being punished by their lord. They demanded that the lord's bailiff should stop interfering in the running of the town.

Thomas Walsingham, 'Historia Anglicana', c.1381

Source G

All men are created equal. Work service had been started by evil men and must be ended. It is against the will of God. Things are not going well in England, nor will they until everything is shared and there are no nobles and no peasants.

John Ball's sermons, described by Thomas Walsingham and Jean Froissart

Source H

John Ball leading the rebels into London

5. What do you think the abbot would say to the villeins (Source D)? Explain your answer.

6. Look at Sources F and G. What reasons can you suggest for Froissart's attitude to Ball?

7. Why do you think that John Ball said that people should take their complaints to the king (Source E)?

8. Why do you think the rebels would trust a priest to be one of their leaders?

After the revolt

When Richard II met the rebels in London he promised them freedom from their lords and an end to work service. He did not keep these promises and was determined to punish the rebels. After all his fine words about freedom, he told them, 'Peasants you were and peasants you shall remain'. He sent his army out with instructions to capture the ringleaders. He ordered his judges to punish them harshly.

The king's orders were carried out with enthusiasm. People were to be taught a lesson. Many villagers, whether they had taken part in the revolt or not, were rounded up and executed. They must know their place and must never be allowed to rebel again.

Source A   Revenge

Judge Tresilian spared no one and took his revenge. Whoever was accused of rebellion, whether rightly or out of hate, was immediately sentenced to death. He ordered some to be beheaded, some to be hung, some to be drawn and quartered. John Ball was himself captured at Coventry and brought to St Albans where he was drawn – his intestines were cut out and burned while he was still alive. He was then hung and his body cut into quarters, so that the four parts of his body could be sent to hang in four different places.

'Chronicle of Henry Knighton', c. 1381

Source B

Lord Thomas Woodstock, Earl of Buckingham, and Lord Thomas Percy, brother of the Earl of Northumberland, were sent to Essex to crush the villagers. Five hundred of the villagers were executed.

Thomas Walsingham, 'Historia Anglicana', c.1381

Source C

Nobles attack unarmed villagers.

Activities

1. Study Source A.

   a) Do you think it is likely that all the accused got a fair trial? Give reasons for your answer.

   b) Why do you think John Ball was executed in this way?

2. Study Source B. Why were the villagers of Essex to be 'crushed'?

3. Look at Source C.

   a) Do you think this was a fair fight? Explain your answer.

   b) What does this source tell us about the nobles' attitude towards the villagers?

The rebels paid dearly for the Great Revolt. The king finally forgave them, but as Source D shows, he wanted a lot in return.

The revolt itself was a failure. The charters giving villagers freedom from their lords were torn up. No land was taken either from the lords or from the church. Change, though, was taking place. Slowly, lords realised that it was easier to pay labourers to work on their land than to make unwilling tenants do work service.

Source E   Work service

It was becoming more and more difficult for lords to make their tenants do work service and it was easier to pay labourers to work for them. By 1500 work service was a thing of the past considered by most people as unnecessary and unjust.

It seems to me that no man should be bound except to God and to his king. He should be set free from any other lord. This is only fair.

Anthony Fitzherbert, 'Boke of Surveying', 1529

Source D   The king forgives

Finally the king took pity on the rebels and ordered that they should be forgiven as long as they did not rebel again.

Everyone was to be given a document showing they were forgiven. However the king wanted to make money out of them. They had to pay 20 shillings for the royal seal that made their document legal.

'Anonimalle Chronicle', c.1381

Source F

The king went to the village of Ospringe in Kent. He asked to see the charters of freedom he had sent to the village agreeing with the rebels' demands. These charters were torn up in front of everybody.

Jean Froissart, c.1381

Checklist

- The Great Revolt took place in 1381.
- Since the Black Death there had been disagreement between lords and tenants over work service and wages.
- The rebels demanded an end to work service and a more equal division of land between people.
- The poll tax of 1380 was hated. The rebels attacked tax collectors and lords before marching to London.
- After the meeting at Smithfield many of the rebels were caught and punished.
- The Great Revolt was a failure. The people's demands were ignored, but gradually work service ended and more people became freemen.

Activities

4. Study Source D. Do you think the king 'took pity' on the peasants?

   Think about the following:

   - the king wanted twenty shillings to forgive a rebel;
   - a labourer might only earn one or two shillings a week;
   - the poll tax had been about two shillings.

5. Read Source F and look back to the Focus.

   a) Do you think the king ever meant to keep his promises to the rebels?

   b) Why do you think the letters were torn up in front of everybody?

6. What are the differences between the view given in Source E and the attitudes of Richard II and the nobles in 1381? What might explain these differences?

12 SCOTLAND, WALES AND IRELAND

1066	William I begins conquest of England.
1067 1075	Norman barons seize land in Wales.

Henry II

1173 1175	Henry II invades Ireland and becomes overlord.
1185	Henry II sends his son John to control the Irish chieftains. The English army is unsuccessful.
1210	John returns to Ireland, builds castles and wins control of the area around Dublin.
1277 1283	Edward I wins control of Wales.
1290 1305	Edward I tries to increase his power in Scotland.
1314	Edward II defeated at Bannockburn by Robert Bruce.
1328	Scottish independence granted by Treaty of Northampton.

Robert Bruce

1394 1399	Richard II tries to conquer Ireland.

Themes

Do you know anyone who has quarrelled with their neighbours? Why did it happen? Was it about land? Or perhaps the neighbours just didn't get on with each other.

England has had many quarrels with her neighbours – Wales, Scotland and Ireland. In the Middle Ages English kings tried to take over and control these neighbouring lands.

This chapter asks the following questions.

- Why did English kings want to control their neighbours?
- How did they attempt to do this?
- How successful were they?

We start with the Battle of Bannockburn in 1314 in which the Scottish king, Robert Bruce, defeated an English army led by Edward II. The English did not try to control Scotland again for nearly 400 years.

Focus Activities

What do you think Edward II and Robert Bruce would have thought and said the day after Bannockburn?

You are a reporter. Write an interview with each of them. You will need to consider:

- the events of the past two days
- their feelings after the battle
- how they see the future of Scotland now.

Bannockburn - Victory for the Scots

Since being crowned King of Scotland in 1306, Robert Bruce had played a successful game of hit-and-run against the English, never facing them in a full-scale battle. He could not afford to do so for he was greatly outnumbered. But now he was forced to stand and fight. Edward II had arrived in Scotland with a force of 20,000 men – including 2,500 heavily armed cavalry and about 5,000 archers. Against this massive army Bruce had only 7,000 troops, including a mere 500 lightly-armed cavalry.

In the late afternoon of 23rd June 1314 the two armies drew up facing each other. Bruce went out to inspect the forward positions. A small crown of gold on his helmet identified him as king. Henry de Bohun, an English knight eager for glory, galloped at Bruce, his lance tilted. The king, on a more nimble horse, neatly sidestepped the English knight, turned in his saddle and 'cleft de Bohun to the brisket' with his axe, splitting him open from head to chest. In the savage fighting which followed the English did not do well. The Scots took heart from their first day of battle.

The English hoped to force the Scots to attack them on the open plain that lay beyond the stream known as Bannockburn. With space for the cavalry to move around and larger numbers they should have the advantage. That night they crossed the muddy stream. It was a hard slog and took most of the night. Spies told Bruce that the enemy was exhausted. At dawn he took his chance for victory and attacked.

The Scottish footsoldiers formed themselves into 'schiltrons' – squares defended with long pikes or spears, that made them look like hedgehogs. Despite repeated attacks the English were unable to break

The English cavalry attack the Scottish schiltrons.

these down. Edward used his archers but it was too late. The English were forced to retreat. The Scots surged forwards chasing the English across the burn. Edward himself managed to escape to Dunbar, where he took a ship for Berwick and safety.

Robert Bruce had won Scotland by right of conquest.

Scotland

The Scottish victory at Bannockburn taught the English a lesson. They did not try to conquer Scotland again. In the Treaty of Northampton, 1328, England finally accepted that Scotland was a separate, independent country.

The problems that led to Bannockburn went back a long time. Even before the Norman conquest the rulers of England had trouble with their northern neighbours. The Romans built walls to keep them out. The people who lived on the borders constantly raided each other's country. Throughout the Middle Ages English chroniclers described attacks by violent and savage people from the north.

Since the Norman conquest English kings had claimed that Scotland belonged to them. They expected Scottish kings to accept them as overlords. That meant they had to pay homage to the English king and promise to obey him.

Source C   The English overlord

King Edward I called the Scottish clergy and nobles before him and extracts were read out from important documents to show how the kings of Scotland had in the past sworn to obey the kings of England and had called them their lords. The Scots clearly did not like this but did not have the power to do anything about it.

'Chronicle of Walter of Guiseborough', 1291

Source A   The Scots (1)

King David of Scotland encouraged his followers to deal most cruelly with the English. They ripped open pregnant women and pulled out unborn babies; they tossed children on the points of their spears and butchered priests at the altar. Wherever the Scots went there was the same scene of horror. Therefore King Stephen invaded Scotland and carried fire and sword through the southern part of King David's country.

'Chronicle of Henry of Huntingdon', 1138

Source B   The Scots (2)

The King of Scotland (David) was a kind and caring prince who was born of religious parents. The natives of Scotland are savage. Swift of foot and lightly armed they make bold and active soldiers. Towards strangers they are cruel and brutal.

Anon., 'The Deeds of Stephen', c.1150

Activities

1. Read Sources A and B.

   a) What are the similarities and differences between these two accounts of King David and the Scots?

   b) How does the writer of Source A explain why Stephen invaded Scotland?

2. Source A was written by an English chronicler. How do you think a Scottish chronicler might have described these events?

3. Use the information on this page to explain why Edward I wanted the Scottish king to obey him and accept him as overlord.

The death of Alexander III of Scotland in 1286 gave Edward I a chance to increase his power in Scotland. However he soon found that the Scots objected to English interference. The events which followed led eventually to the Battle of Bannockburn (Source D).

Source E

Edward I, King of England, sent letters to John Balliol, King of Scotland, asking him for some of the finest soldiers in his army to fight in Edward's war against France. But the Scots, having made a treaty of friendship with Philip IV, King of France, refused. They said that neither their king nor themselves had to obey the King of England's wishes or commands.

'Chronicle of Walter of Guiseborough', 1295

Source F

Robert Bruce and his wife

Source D   Events leading to Bannockburn

1286   Alexander III of Scotland was killed in a riding accident leaving no heir. In the next four years 13 rivals claimed the throne.

1290   Edward I of England was asked by the Scottish nobles to help choose between the rivals. Edward chose John Balliol because he promised to accept him as overlord.

1295   John Balliol refused Edward's order to fight against the French and rebelled against him. The rebellion was crushed and Balliol taken prisoner. Edward I then ruled Scotland himself.

1297   William Wallace, a Scottish knight, began another rebellion which lasted until 1305 when he was captured and executed.

1306   Robert Bruce had himself crowned King of Scotland and began raids against the English.

1314   The Battle of Bannockburn – Edward II was defeated after trying to conquer Scotland.

3. Study Source D.

    a) In what ways did the English try to control what happened in Scotland between 1290 and 1314?

    b) What did the Scots do about these attempts to control them?

4. Read Source E.

    a) What reasons can you suggest for Balliol's refusal to send troops?

    b) Has the Scottish attitude to the English king changed from the one given in Source C? Explain your answer.

5. Draw a picture of Edward I and Robert Bruce. Add 'thought bubbles' and write in what each might think of the other's country.

The conquest of Wales

In the eighth century an English king, Offa of Mercia, built a huge earthwork, or dyke, to keep the Welsh out. The neighbouring people did not get on.

The Welsh were united by their language and customs but divided by their mountains. By the end of the twelfth century there were three main principalities in Wales (areas ruled by a prince) – Gwynedd in the north, around Mount Snowdon, Powys in the centre and Deheubarth in the south and west. English kings expected Welsh princes to accept them as overlords. However the Welsh had other ideas.

William the Conqueror had strengthened English defences by granting land along the Welsh border to powerful barons. These 'Marcher Lords' built a string of castles from Chester in the north to Chepstow in the south. They carved out large areas of land for themselves on the Welsh side of the border.

Source A The Welsh (1)

The Welsh people are fierce rather than strong. They are all trained in war, spending much of their time doing military training. They love freedom and are determined to defend their country. For these they fight, for these suffer hardships, for these they will take up their weapons and willingly lose their lives.

'Chronicle of Gerald of Wales' (a Welsh monk), c.1250

Source B The Welsh (2)

In May, the Welsh burst forth from their dens like shrews from holes, raising fires everywhere. They spared neither church nor clergy, and those noble women and girls who had sought peace and safety were burned along with the churches themselves. King Henry III sent Hubert de Burgh to stop the attacks. However, the Welsh continued to cross the border and attack the lands of the English barons.

'Chronicle of Roger of Wendover' (an English monk), 1231

Source C Wales

lands captured and controlled by English barons by 1250

lands belong to Gwynedd in 1247

lands conquered by Gwynedd, 1247-67

lands of other Welsh princes who supported Gwynedd in 1267

castles built by Edward I, 1290s

castles built by marcher lords, 1066-1300

Activities

1. Read Sources A and B.

   a) In what ways do they agree about the Welsh people?

   b) In what ways do they disagree?

   c) How might these differences be explained?

2. Copy the map in Source C. Draw a line to join up the castles built by Marcher Lords. What does this suggest about the trouble spots in the eleventh and twelfth centuries?

Llywelyn, Prince of Gwynedd, gained the support of the other Welsh princes to rule all of Wales. He accepted Henry III as his overlord but later refused to pay homage to Edward I. Border raiding turned into open rebellion. Edward took an army to Wales in 1276 but Llywelyn hid in the mountains around Snowdon, his longbowmen keeping the English at bay. Edward cut off his food supply from the island of Anglesey and starved him into surrender. Llywelyn was allowed to keep Gwynedd but had to give up his other lands.

In 1282, Llywelyn's brother, Daffyd, started another rebellion. Llywelyn joined in but was killed in battle. His head was put on show at the Tower of London. In 1283 Daffyd was captured. He was dragged behind a horse, then hanged, drawn and quartered – the parts of his body being sent to four different English cities. His sons were imprisoned in Bristol and his daughters, like Llywelyn's only child, were sent to an English convent.

To prevent further trouble, Edward built castles in North Wales. Most were 'concentric' in design with two circular walls, one inside the other, and massive towers at the entrance and corners of the keep. From here archers could shower the enemy with arrows. Each tower could defend itself even if the others were captured.

Source F   Beaumaris Castle

A concentric castle in North Wales – it was started but never completed.

Source D   Llywelyn (1)

Here lies the scourge of England,
Snowdonia's guardian sure,
Llywelyn, Prince of Wales,
In character most pure,
Of modern kings the jewel,
Of kings long past the flower,
For kings to come a pattern,
Radiant in lawful power.
Anon.

Source E   Llywelyn (2)

Here lies the prince of errors,
A traitor and a thief,
A flaring, flaming firebrand,
The malefactors'* chief.
The wild Welsh evil genius,
Who sought the good to kill,
Dregs of the faithless Trojans*,
And source of every ill.

* Malefactor - criminal
* The Trojans were believed to be the
  ancestors of the Welsh.

Anon.

3. Read Sources D and E. One of these poems was written by a Welsh monk, the other by an English monk. Who do you think wrote which poem? Explain your answer.

4. Study Sources C and F.

    a) Use Source F to draw a rough ground plan of a concentric castle. Why would it be so difficult to capture?

    b) Concentric castles were very expensive to build. What does this tell us about Edward's determination to keep control of Wales?

    c) Why do you think Edward chose to build the castles at the places shown in Source C?

    d) What reasons can you suggest to explain why Beaumaris Castle (Source F) was never completed?

Ireland

A trip to Ireland was not undertaken lightly in medieval times. Boats were small and the Irish Sea was rough. From the time of Henry II in 1171, to Richard II in 1399, several English kings showed an interest in Ireland. But their attempts at conquest and control met with little success.

Ireland was divided into 'kingdoms'. Rival 'kings' fought each other for control of the country and sometimes looked to English barons for help. In 1166 Dermot MacMurrough, 'king' of Leinster, asked Henry II to help him fight Rory O'Connor of Connacht. Henry gave English barons permission to help but they simply seized land for themselves. In 1171 Henry went to Ireland himself. The Irish 'kings' and the English barons in Ireland agreed to accept Henry as their overlord but he had little control over the country. The same applied to King John, who built castles in Ireland but was largely ignored by the Irish.

Ireland west of the 'Pale' (Source B) remained outside English control.

Source A   Irishmen

Source B   Ireland

This map shows 'kingdoms' of rival ruling families. The Pale was the area around Dublin where English barons took land and settled – this was the only part of Ireland the English were able to control.

Source C   Henry II's visit to Ireland

When the Irish understood that the King of England only intended to bring peace and that he did not encourage crimes, nor sentence anyone to death without good cause, they met him to discuss peace. Since they had trouble keeping control themselves and since their fathers had killed each other in civil wars, the Irish handed over power to Henry II so that they should have peace.

Ralph of Diceto (an English monk), 'Images of History', 1172

Source D   Irish kings complain

The Irish have become wicked by mixing with the English. Different from us in the language they speak and the way they behave, all hope of staying peaceful with them is out of the question.

Letter to Pope John XXII, c.1317

Richard II was one of the few English kings to make a serious attempt to gain control of Ireland. In 1394 he defeated the Irish 'kings'. He left Robert de Vere, an English noble, in charge but English control was soon lost.

Richard went back to Ireland in 1399. This time he had little success. He returned quickly to England when he found his enemies were plotting to overthrow him. Perhaps this helps to explain why later English kings did not travel to Ireland very often.

Source E

Art MacMurrough, the 'king' of Leinster, and his soldiers (on the right) attack Richard II's soldiers, 1399.

Activities

1. Source A was drawn by an English monk. What do you think it tells us about how the English saw the Irish?

2. Study Sources B and C. How successful were English kings in controlling Ireland? Can you suggest reasons for this?

3. Read Sources C and D.
   a) What change do they show in Irish attitudes towards the English?
   b) How might this change be explained?

4. How does a picture like Source E help us to understand the relations between England and Ireland in the 14th century and the difficulties foreign armies faced in Ireland?

5. How do you account for the similarities in English chroniclers' descriptions of the Scots, Welsh and Irish in this chapter?

Checklist

- The kings of England tried to control Scotland, Wales and Ireland. They feared attack from warlike neighbours; they wanted more land and power; and they wanted to make sure that no one could threaten their position.

- Scotland fought against English control and won its independence.

- Wales was taken over by Edward I and castles were built to keep the Welsh in order.

- English kings made several attempts to gain control of Ireland, but very little of the country was ever actually ruled by England.

- Much of our information about Scotland, Wales and Ireland in the Middle Ages comes from English chroniclers.

13 BRITAIN AND THE WIDER WORLD

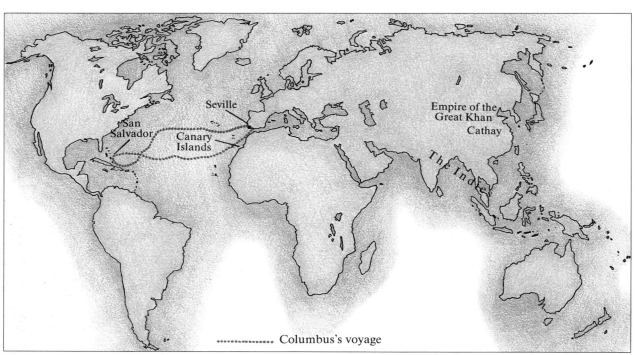

·············· Columbus's voyage

Columbus's voyage

Themes

For most medieval people the centre of their world was the village or town in which they lived. Unless they were traders, or went to war, they would probably spend almost all their lives there.

This did not mean that people knew nothing about the outside world. Those who travelled learned a great deal about distant lands. The links between the peoples of Europe grew closer during the Middle Ages. Their languages were similar, their royal families married one another and above all they shared the same religion – Christianity.

This chapter asks the following questions.

- How did medieval people see the world?
- What were Britain's links with Europe?
- What was Christendom?

We start in 1493 when Christopher Columbus returned from a voyage of discovery. He had tried to find a shorter route to China and the Indies by sailing west rather than east. The Focus is based on extracts from Columbus's account of his voyage.

Focus Activities

Read the passage opposite and look at the map above.

1. a) Where did Columbus plan to go?
    b) Where did he actually go?

2. Why do you think there was great excitement on Columbus's return? Think about what his voyage would have meant to Queen Isabella and the church.

3. Write an account of the voyage as it might have been seen by an ordinary sailor on the voyage.

Voyage to the 'new world'

Seville, Spain   June 1493

Greetings from the High Admiral of the Ocean and Viceroy of the Western Indies! For that is what I have become as a result of my amazing voyage across the western seas in search of India, Cathay and the Court of the Great Khan. I carried a letter for the Khan from Queen Isabella of Spain, who paid for my voyage.

I sailed in the Santa Maria, with two other ships, the Nina and the Pinta. Fear of the unknown meant that I had to handle the crews very carefully to avoid a mutiny – they might refuse to obey my commands. As we left the Canary Islands and struck out into the vast empty seas in our tiny ships, the first signs of panic showed themselves. Some sailors wept and begged me to turn back, sure they would never see their families again. Cowards all! None had my courage, my determination or my vision!

About a month after we set out we were averaging over 100 km a day. I lied to the sailors and told them it was less because they had never sailed so far from land before. I kept them busy looking for land. There were several false alarms when banks of low cloud were spotted.

Then, in October, one crewman, Roderigo, sighted land. He has claimed the reward I offered, but I shall keep it myself – this was *my* venture. I named this island San Salvador. We sailed round many such islands observing their great beauty – brightly-coloured parrots and other wildlife and lush, green vegetation. We searched for spices and gold and tried to communicate with the naked natives we met. I have brought back samples of many things we found – including six of the natives. I think they will make very good slaves.

Title page of Columbus's account of his voyage

Everyone here is very excited at my great achievements. I have found a western route to the Indies and claimed many lands for Spain. The great adventure is over – or is it just beginning? The way is open for us to find their hidden gold and to bring Christianity to their heathen peoples.

The world

Some medieval people travelled widely. Kings, soldiers, traders, and pilgrims went on long journeys that might take years to complete. There were few methods of travel. Ships were so small that today they would be called boats. The fastest way of travelling was by horse. European people only knew about a small part of the world. They did not know that America and Australia existed. Africa had not been explored apart from a few areas around the northern coasts. Traders travelled overland to China, Japan and Eastern Russia, but knew very little about them.

Source B   Round or flat earth?

Men may yet prove that it is possible to go by ship all around the world. It seems to simple and unlearned men that people may not go to the other side of the earth because they would fall off, but this may not be.

Sir John de Mandeville, 14th century

Source C   A religious view of the world

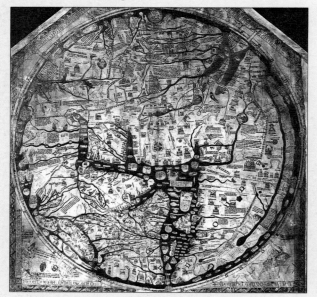

Mappe Mundi, c.1300

Jerusalem is shown at the centre of the world. According to the *Bible*, 'Thus said the Lord, "This is Jerusalem, I have put it in the middle of the world"'. This type of map was intended to show the world as God planned it, not as people knew it to be.

Source A

Map of England, Scotland and Wales drawn by the English chronicler, Matthew Paris, c.1250

Activities

1. a) Draw your own map of Britain from memory.

    b) Compare your map with Source A. Which is more accurate? In what ways?

    c) What advantages did you have over Matthew Paris in drawing your map?

2. Does Sir John de Mandeville (Source B) believe the world is round or flat? Explain your answer.

3. Study Source C.

    a) How accurate is this map?

    b) Why do you think it was drawn in this way?

4. Most overseas travellers followed trade routes that were well known. Why do you think this was?

Travellers brought back much information about the world and the creatures that lived in it. Some of this information was very reliable. Thomas Walsingham, for example, wrote an accurate description of dolphins. However other information was less accurate. Because they had no cameras, travellers could only describe what they had seen in words and sketches. It is not always easy to describe something to people who have never seen anything like it before.

5. Look at Source D.
   a) What **should** de Mandeville have written for the artist to have been able to draw a more accurate giraffe?
   b) Work in pairs. Each invent a creature. Draw and colour it but **do not** show the picture to your partner. Write a description of it and give it to your partner. Now draw each other's creature from the description. Compare pictures when you have finished. How accurate were you? Why?

6. Compare Sources E and F.
   a) In what ways are they similar and in what ways different?
   b) Are these sources as silly as they first appear? Explain your answer.

Source D   A giraffe

Picture drawn from a 14th century description by Sir John de Mandeville

Source E

In one of the islands in the Far East are giants, hideous to look at – they have only one eye in the middle of the forehead and they eat nothing but raw flesh and fish. In another isle to the south lives a small evil tribe who have no heads and their eyes are in their shoulders. In another isle there are people with lips so big that they can cover their faces with them as they sleep in the sun. In another isle there are people with ears which hang down to their knees.

Sir John de Mandeville, 14th century

Source F   People from far off lands

A picture from a fourteenth century book

Britain and Europe

Look at the map below. Britain is an island on the edge of Europe, separated from the rest of the continent by a narrow channel of sea. But this does not mean that England was cut off from the rest of Europe. Over the centuries many invaders from Europe attacked and settled in Britain – Romans from Italy, Saxons from north Germany and Vikings from Denmark and Norway. After the Norman conquest there were close ties between England and France. Throughout the Middle Ages English kings held lands in France and fought wars to keep them.

The story of Britain and Europe was not all conflict and warfare. As the map below shows, there were close trading links. From Roman times onwards England had grown rich from exports of wool to the continent. Throughout the Middle Ages merchants made long and often dangerous journeys to buy and sell many kinds of goods. In England there was a big demand for exotic silks and spices from the hot lands of southern Europe, the Middle East and Asia.

Source A

Merchants came from every part of the world. The Arabian sends gold*; from the Yemen spices and incense*; from Babylon palm oil*; precious stones from the Nile*; from Russia and Norway furs; from China purple silk. The French come with their wines.

(*from the Middle East)

William FitzStephen, 'Description of the City of London', c.1170

Source B

Wool was England's main export during Edward II's reign. Most went to the great cloth-manufacturing towns of the Low Countries (Belgium and Holland). Many of England's other exports – fish, corn, cheese, hides and lead – went to Gascony, which, under English rule, used more and more of its land to grow vines. Most of the wine produced from these vines was shipped to England. More than 5 million gallons a year were drunk by people of all social classes, from the king to all but his poorest subjects.

Adapted from E. Hallam (editor), 'The Age of Chivalry', 1987

Source C British trade with Europe and the Middle East

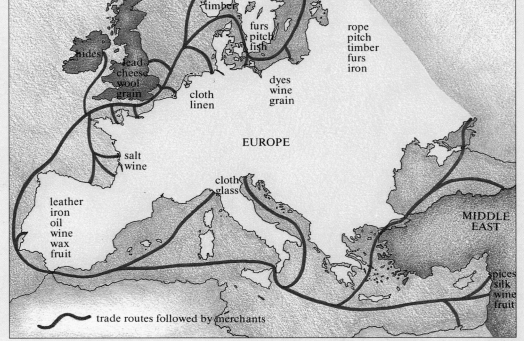

fish
timber
furs
pitch
fish
rope
pitch
timber
furs
iron
dyes
wine
grain
hides
hides
lead
cheese
wool
grain
cloth
linen
EUROPE
salt
wine
cloth
glass
leather
iron
oil
wine
wax
fruit
MIDDLE
EAST
spices
silk
wine
fruit

~ trade routes followed by merchants

Every English king between 1199 and 1461 married a French princess or a French noblewoman. But marriage did not bring peace between the two kingdoms. The kings of England and France were rivals for land and power. This often led to war between the two countries.

Within 100 years of the Norman conquest Henry II held most of France – more than the French king himself. However most of these lands, including Normandy, were lost in wars with the French during King John's reign. By the time Edward III came to the throne in 1327 only Gascony and a small part of northern France remained in English hands.

War with France broke out again in 1337. It lasted so long that it became known as the Hundred Years War. Fighting did not go on all the time – there were many years of peace between the battles. In the early years the English won some spectacular victories and captured most of France. But by the end of the war, England had lost all her French lands except Calais.

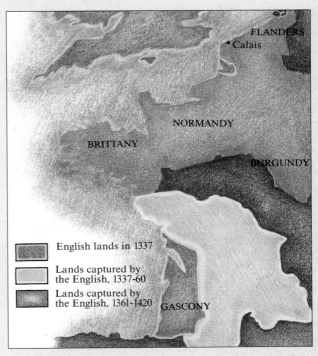

Source D   English lands in France, 1337-1420

English lands in 1337

Lands captured by the English, 1337-60

Lands captured by the English, 1361-1420

FLANDERS
• Calais
NORMANDY
BRITTANY
BURGUNDY
GASCONY

Source E   Causes of the Hundred Years War

- Edward III was young and brave – he liked fighting and wanted the glory and excitement of a war with France.
- The French threatened to take over Gascony and stop the wine trade with England.
- Edward III was the grandson of King Philip IV of France. He claimed that he was the rightful King of France.
- The French threatened the English wool trade with Flanders – English ships carrying wool were attacked in the Channel.
- Edward III was trying to conquer Scotland – the French promised to help the Scots against Edward.

Source F

The English will never love or honour their king unless he is victorious and loves fighting. The English war against their neighbours, especially those who are richer than themselves. They thoroughly enjoy battles and slaughter and they are always jealous of other people's riches.

Jean Froissart, late 14th century

Activities

1. Study Sources A, B and C.
   a) Where did most of the goods brought to England come from:
      - the Middle East
      - Europe
      - other parts of the world?
   b) You are a merchant in London selling goods from different parts of the world. Design a poster advertising your goods and where they came from. Use pictures as well as words.

2. Why was Gascony so important to England (Source B)?

3. Look at Source E. Put the reasons why Edward III went to war with France in order of importance. Why have you chosen this order?

4. Does Source F provide a satisfactory explanation for England's wars with France? Give reasons for your answer.

Christendom

Although there were many things which divided the peoples of Western Europe, there was one thing which united them – their religion. They were all part of Christendom. They all shared the same religious leader – the pope.

The areas around Constantinople and Greece – the Eastern Empire – had their own form of Christianity. However the rest of Europe took its lead from the Bishop of Rome, the pope. He was the successor to Jesus's disciple, St Peter. Although there were sometimes quarrels and splits within the church, most people in medieval Europe saw themselves as part of Christendom.

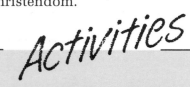

1. Look at Source A. What does this statue tell us about the importance of the pope to medieval Christians?

2. How do Sources A and B add to your understanding of what Christendom was?

Source A   St Peter, the first pope

The pope was the leader of Christendom.

Source B Christendom

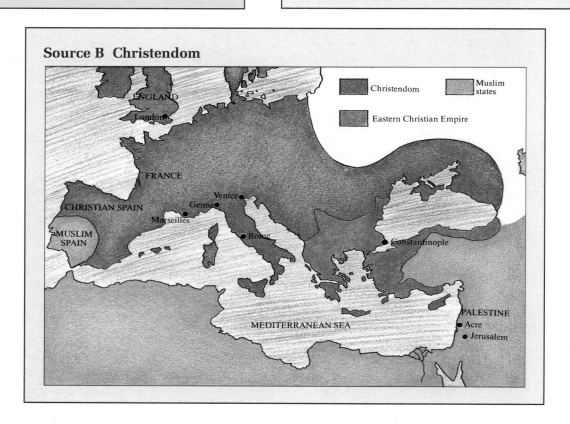

The Crusades

People really felt a part of Christendom when there was conflict between Christians and the outside, non-Christian world.

All good Christians wanted to go on a pilgrimage – a journey to a holy place – before they died. The most important places were in the Holy Land – Palestine – where Jesus had lived and died.

Jerusalem in Palestine is a sacred city to Muslims, Jews and Christians. Since the 7th century the Holy Land had been under Muslim rule. Christian pilgrims were still allowed to visit but this stopped in the 11th century when Turkish Muslims overran the area and Christians were tortured and killed.

Christians in Western Europe were horrified. They joined together in a series of Crusades, or 'wars of the cross', to win back the Holy Land for Christendom. Over a period of nearly 200 years various armies from England, France and Germany tried to recapture Palestine. They had little success. In 1291 the Muslims captured Acre, the last Christian city in the Holy Land.

Source A

Pope Urban II asking soldiers to fight the First Crusade in 1095

Source B

Let all Christians know that news has come from the east that the Church of the Holy Sepulchre in Jerusalem has been destroyed from roof to foundations at the hands of the pagans (non-Christians). The whole world is in mourning and the people tremble, breathing deep sighs. With the Lord's help we intend to kill all those enemies. God has promised that whoever dies for the sake of Christ will gain another life which he will never lose.

Anon., late 11th century

Activities

1. a) Study Sources A and B. From what you know about the power and influence of the medieval church, why do you think people were prepared to go to war against the Muslims?
   b) Can you think of any other reasons why they might go to fight in the Holy Land?

2. How do you think that Muslims in Jerusalem would have felt about what was said in Source B?

3. Do you think Christendom still exists? Give reasons for your answer.

Checklist

- By the end of the Middle Ages Europeans were exploring distant lands and discovering 'new worlds'.

- There was a great deal of trade between the countries of Europe. There was also trade with the Middle East, India and China.

- There were wars between England and France throughout the Middle Ages.

- The Christian countries of Western Europe were known as Christendom.

- Christians and Muslims fought a series of wars – the Crusades – for control of the Holy Land.

An illuminated manuscript

The Tower of London – a royal palace

Themes

Historians can learn a lot about people from their buildings, clothes, art, music, language, writing and poetry. These things are all part of the 'culture' of a people.

This chapter examines the culture of the Middle Ages. It looks at:

- Buildings
- Art
- Language
- Storytelling and music.

It asks what we can learn from culture about the way people lived, what they thought and what was important to them.

The Middle Ages was a time of sharp contrasts. On the one hand there were magnificent cathedrals and fine manor houses, on the other, small and humble peasant houses clustered round the village green. The rich paraded round court in expensive silks and velvets while the poor wore simple woollen garments. Not many people could read or write and only a small number owned books. But a few spent their lives producing the most beautiful books which only the rich could afford.

The Focus describes a visit by Will, a young man from York, to the court of King Edward III in London.

Focus Activities

Read the passage opposite.

1. Using the definition of culture in the first paragraph of the *Themes* box, make a list of examples of culture mentioned in the letter.

2. The way a person dressed showed how important they were. Explain this using an example from Will's letter.

3. Do you think you would have enjoyed a day at King Edward III's court? Give reasons for your answer.

Life at court

Dear Richard,

How glad I am now for all those beatings I suffered when I was a student. My teacher, the monk, Brother James, knew I was lazy. But for him I would not have learned to read and write. I would not have been able to write to you like this and describe the wonders of the capital city and the court of our king, Edward III.

London really is a wonderful place. The houses of the merchants at home in York are small and unimportant compared to those here. And the palaces! They are so fine and grand I think a man could wander all day in one and not find his way out.

The noblemen at court and their ladies dress very finely in silks and velvets of many colours. I have been warned though, that not being a nobleman, the lining for my winter cloak should only be made of coney (rabbit fur). Not that I could afford miniver (white fur) anyway!

The king and his courtiers usually speak French. But I have been pleased to find many that also speak English. However, their English is very different from ours. They use different words – and the accent! It's hard to understand them at times.

On St George's Day there were great celebrations. The weather was fine and

Lords and ladies at court

a huge tent was put up in the grounds of the palace. It looked very grand, decorated with flowers, shields, flags and banners. Knights appeared in armour and everyone wore their finest jewellery.

The entertainment started early. The highlight was certainly the poet, Geoffrey Chaucer, who read his latest poem. The king was so impressed he gave him a supply of wine for life! There was also a play and a magic show. Musicians finished the day by playing music for us to dance.

Your brother,

Will

Homes

We all know who's got the best houses today – people with money. The same was true of the Middle Ages. This section looks at medieval homes. Most of those that have survived belonged to wealthy families.

Bodiam Castle (Source A), built in Richard III's reign, was the home of a rich and powerful nobleman. The house shown in Source B belonged to Thomas Paycocke, a wealthy cloth merchant, who died in 1461. Penshurst Place in Sussex (Source C) was the home of the local lord of the manor. Each of these buildings had a hall where the family dined and where the servants usually slept at night. The family had their own bedrooms and living rooms on the first floor. Homes of this size usually had a chapel too.

Most people in the Middle Ages lived in houses like the one pictured in Source D. This is an artist's impression – the house has not survived. Here the family slept in one room. There was no chimney – smoke from the fire escaped through a hole in the roof. Farm animals were often kept in the house for safekeeping – and they helped to keep the family warm during the long winter months.

Source A   A nobleman's home

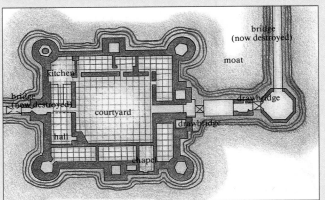

Bodiam Castle, Sussex

Source B   A merchant's home

Thomas Paycocke's house, Coggeshall, Essex

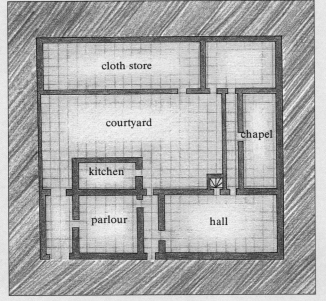

Source C   A lord's home

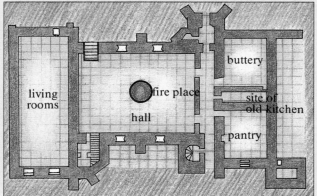

Penshurst Place, Sussex

Source D   A peasant's home

Activities

1. There was a wide gap between rich and poor in the Middle Ages. What evidence do homes provide to support this statement?

2. Why do you think homes like those shown in Sources A-C have survived while those like the one in Source D have not?

3. How do you think you would feel living in a peasant's home (Source D)? Do you think a medieval peasant would have felt the same way? Why?

4. Look at the advertisement opposite for a present day house. If there had been estate agents in the Middle Ages how might they have advertised Penshurst Place (Source C) and the cottage in Source D? Write an advertisement for each. You may use drawings if you wish.

FOR SALE

Modern detached house in quiet position with medium-sized garden. The house is built in brick with tiled roof, double glazed windows and central heating.

On the ground floor there is a hallway, large lounge and fully-fitted kitchen with gas cooker.

On the first floor there are one large and two medium-sized bedrooms. Separate bathroom and toilet are provided.

Offers invited. View by appointment.

89

Art

Most art in the Middle Ages was religious.

Source A shows a page from a book which was written and painted by a medieval monk. The page is decorated with pictures and bright colourful designs. These books are known as 'illuminated manuscripts'. Many were produced in the Middle Ages. Sometimes the pictures showed Bible stories, sometimes scenes from everyday life. Only very wealthy families could afford books like this.

Noblemen sometimes paid artists to paint pictures specially for them. These paintings usually showed religious scenes. For example, Richard II paid for a painting of the Three Kings visiting the baby Jesus. Artists often included the nobleman's family in the picture.

Ordinary people could not afford works of art but they would have seen them when they went to church. Churches were full of beautiful paintings and carvings in wood and stone. Bible stories were explained in pictures on the walls (see the 'doom painting' on page 36). Coloured (stained) glass was used to make pictures in the windows.

Source A   An illuminated manuscript

Source B   A stained glass window

This window from the church at Long Melford, Suffolk, shows a noblewoman who lived nearby.

Activities

1. Why do you think that religion was so important in medieval art?

2. Why do you think pictures were so important to people in the Middle Ages?

3. a) Describe the picture shown in Source B.
   b) Why do you think this lady's family paid for the window to be made?

4. Design a stained glass window with yourself as the main subject. What clothes will you wear? What designs will you use? What other things could you include to make the window special to you?

5. Study the illuminated manuscript in Source A. Design your own illustration – perhaps of a poem, or even your name. In the first letter draw scenes from school life.

Language

Would your great-grandparents understand the way you speak today? Yes and no. New words and ways of pronouncing them are always creeping into everyday speech, almost without us realising it.

In the same way the English spoken in 1500 was very different from that spoken by the Saxons in 1066. We know little about medieval English because it was not often written down. We do know that each area of the country had its own dialect or way of speaking. And we know that the main version of English grew out of the dialect spoken in the East Midlands and Southeast.

The Normans who conquered England in 1066 spoke a French dialect. Latin was used in church and in the law courts. But most people – the ordinary villagers and townspeople – still spoke English. However, many French and Latin words and phrases came into everyday English speech.

By 1500 things had changed. English was used in law courts and manor houses up and down the country and even at the king's court. The first English translation of the Bible had appeared. Only a few very well educated churchmen could read Latin. Poems and stories were being printed in English. It was French and Latin that were unusual now.

Source A   French to English

John Cornwal, a grammar school teacher, changed from teaching in French to teaching in English; and Richard Pencrych learned that way of teaching from him, so that now, in the year of our lord one thousand, three hundred, four score and five (1385), in the reign of the second King Richard, in all the grammar schools in England children are learning in English and translating Latin into English instead of French.

Ranulf Higden, 'Polychronicon', Trevisa's translation, 1385

Source B   Some Norman words

Source C   An English poem

Medieval English

Ye knowe ek that in forme of speche is chaunge
Withinne a thousand yeer, and wordes tho
That hadden pris, now wonder nyce and straunge
Us thinketh hem, and yet thei spake hem so.

Modern English

You know too that forms of speech change over a thousand years, and words that had a certain meaning, no wonder we think them strange and yet they spoke them so.

Geoffrey Chaucer, 'Troilus and Criseyde', late 14th century

Activities

1. What changes in language and education are mentioned in Source A?
2. Why do you think English replaced French and Latin?
3. Look at Source B. Make a list of words you have learned in French lessons which are similar to English words with the same meaning.
4. a) Historians think that medieval English was spelt the way it was spoken. Read the passage from Chaucer in Source C out loud.
   b) Is modern English spelt the way it sounds?
5. Make a list of words and phrases used today which your great-grandparents would not understand. Why wouldn't they understand them?

Storytelling

Most people in the Middle Ages liked a good story. They entertained each other by telling stories. They listened to minstrels who set stories to music and poets who put stories in verse.

Geoffrey Chaucer was one of the first poets to write in English. His best known poems were the *Canterbury Tales* which describe a group of pilgrims setting out from London to visit Thomas Becket's tomb at Canterbury. The poems also retell the stories told by each pilgrim during the journey. Chaucer's poems were so popular that he was asked by Edward III to read them at court.

Source A

Chaucer reading his poems at court

Source B

Pilgrims leaving Canterbury. They told each other stories as they travelled.

Source C Chaucer's knight

There was a knight, a valiant (brave) man,
Who, from the time when he had first begun
To venture out, had loved chivalry,
Truth and honour, freedom and courtesy.
He had proved his worth in his lord's wars,
In which he had ridden as fast as any man,
Both in christendom and in heathen lands,
And he had always been honoured for his valour.

Chaucer, 'Prologue to the Canterbury Tales', c.138, translated by Nevill Coghill

Activities

1. Why do you think Chaucer was reading his poem aloud to the court (Source A)?

2. Look at Source B. Why do you think storytelling was popular with pilgrims?

3. Source C is a work of fiction – Chaucer made it up. What are the advantages and disadvantages of this type of source to historians?

4. It has been said that storytelling today is a 'dying art'. Why might this be so?

Music and plays

Most medieval music was written for performance in church. However, the Middle Ages also had its pop songs and dance music. Stories were often put to music and sung by travelling minstrels. Singing over a mug of ale was a popular pastime. Since there were no recordings, all music was played and sung 'live'.

'Miracle' plays were another form of popular entertainment. A performance drew large crowds. In towns they were organised by the guilds (see pages 30-31). The plays told stories from the Bible or about saints, in everyday language.

Source B   A miracle play

We are poor husbandmen (farmers) that walk on the moor,

In faith! We'll be lucky to keep our own doors (homes).
No wonder, as things stand, that we are so poor,
Our lands lie fallow as a cold stone floor,
You know!

We are crippled with toil,
And crushed to the soil,
And taxed 'til we fall ...

'Second Wakefield Miracle Play'

Source A   A popular song

Summer is acoming in, loudly sing
    cuckoo,
Groweth seed and bloweth mead and
    springs the wood anew. Sing cuckoo,
Ewe now bleateth after lamb, low'th
    after calf the cow,
Bullock boundeth, roebuck soundeth,
    merry sing cuckoo,
Cuckoo, cuckoo. Well may you sing
    cuckoo, nor cease from singing now.

'Sumer is icumen in', c.1240

Checklist

- Historians can learn a lot about people from their culture.

- There was a wide gap between rich and poor in the Middle Ages. This can be seen clearly from their homes.

- Most medieval art was based on religious themes.

- English gradually replaced French as the language of the nobility and Latin as the language of the law courts.

- Storytelling, music and plays were the main forms of popular entertainment.

Activities

1. Look at Source A.

   a) Why do you think people in the Middle Ages would enjoy this song?

   b) Would songs about cuckoos and farm animals be suitable for pop music today? Explain your answer.

2. Look at Source B. Why do you think these lines would mean a lot to ordinary people?

15 CONCLUSION

The end of the Middle Ages

The world is always changing. Small changes over a long period can add up to large changes. Often we only notice this when we look back. Sometimes a single invention or discovery can have a very big effect on people's whole way of life. Think how the aeroplane, television and computer have changed the way we live this century.

Looking back from 1500, people may not have thought life had changed much since 1066. In some ways they were right. Most people still worked the land and this would be the same for the next three hundred years.

However, the Middle Ages did bring important changes which still affect our lives today.

First, more **freedom**. The beginnings of parliament meant that a larger number of people were beginning to have more say in the way the country was run. The breakdown of the feudal system also meant more freedom. Burgesses bought charters which gave them

Source A   New weapons

Gunpowder and cannon meant castle walls could be knocked down easily. Nobles built comfortable manor houses to live in instead.

Source B   New machines

The printing press meant more knowledge and information were available to those who could afford it.

freedom from work service. Many peasants were becoming wage labourers which freed them from their lords.

Second, more **rights** and greater **justice**. Many of the rights granted in Magna Carta – for example trial by jury – are part of our modern way of life. The courts started by Henry II can be seen as the beginnings of today's system of justice. They steadily replaced the barons' courts.

Third, **urbanisation** – the growth of towns and cities. Many new towns grew up in the Middle Ages. Today most of us live in towns and cities.

Source C   New lands

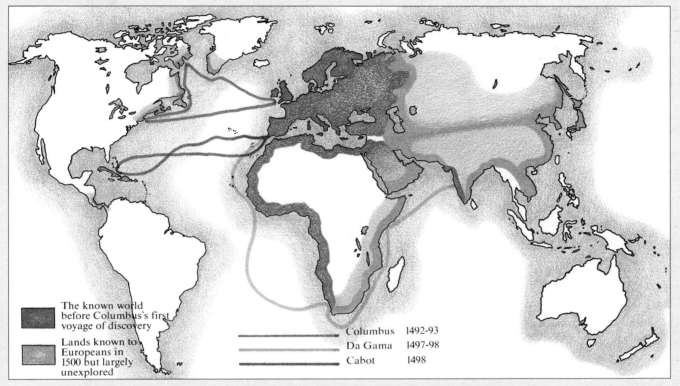

The known world before Columbus's first voyage of discovery

Lands known to Europeans in 1500 but largely unexplored

Columbus   1492-93
Da Gama   1497-98
Cabot   1498

Exploration meant new goods, knowledge and opportunities – especially for the growing merchant class.

Fourth, the growth of **manufacturing.** The craft guilds that grew up in the Middle Ages began the organised production of all sorts of goods, from shoes, bread and furniture to cloth and glass. This paved the way for the industrial revolution of the late eighteenth and early nineteenth centuries and today's factories.

Fifth, **discovery** and **exploration.** Voyages of discovery began to change people's view of the world. This has continued to the present day with exploration of the sea bed and outer space.

Sixth, new **inventions.** New machines and new weapons continue to change our lives.

Changes which began and developed in the Middle Ages have altered the way we live, the way we think and the way we see the world.

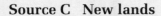

Activities

1. In what ways do you think that television has changed people's lives? List as many ways as you can.

2. Study Sources A–C. Make a list of the changes shown. Against each, explain how it might affect people's lives at the time.

3. It is the early sixteenth century. You have just heard a rumour that Columbus did not find a different route to the east but in fact discovered a vast new land. You wonder how this will affect your life. What would you want to know about the new world? What questions would you ask about it?

Acknowledgements

Cover   Caroline Waring-Collins (Art Direction)

Illustrations   Caroline Waring-Collins (Art Direction)

Computer generated artwork   Elaine Marie Cox (Picatype)

Page design   Andrew Allen

Typing   Ingrid Hamer

Library assistance   Rosemary Campbell-Blair, Sandringham School Library

Trialling material   Mr Redmond and pupils of Ormskirk Grammar School and Mr Platford and pupils of St Bede's High School, Ormskirk

Picture credits

Ashmolean Museum, Oxford pp. 5 (t), 8, 10 (b), 44, 70 (t, b); Bodleian Library, University of Oxford p. 76 (Ms. Laud Misc. 720, fol. 226v); British Library pp. 4 (b, inset), 18 (tr, b), 19 (tr, ml, mr, b), 20 (t, m), 21, 30, 31, 33, 35 (b), 37 (tr), 41, 45, 48, 51, 56 (b), 57, 63, 67, 77, 93 and cover; Cambridge University Committee for Aerial Photography pp. 26 (t), 64, 75, 86 (b); Syndics of Cambridge University Library p. 4 (b); President and Fellows of Corpus Christi College, Oxford p. 17 (l); C.M. Dixon pp. 24 (t), 25; Fotomas Index pp. 6 (t, m, b), 9, 10 (t), 12, 92 (b); Sonia Halliday pp. 37 (bl, br); Michael Holford pp. 13 (t, b), 34, 72, 88 (t); Hulton Picture Company p. 43; A.F. Kersting pp. 20 (b), 24 (b), 32 (t, b), 35 (t), 39, 50, 81 (b), 84 (t), 85 (b), 89 (tl), 90 (b); Mansell Collection pp. 11, 18 (t, l), 28, 54 (t, b); Trustees of the National Library of Scotland/Sir David Ogilvy p. 73; Peter Newark's Pictures p. 15; Norton Priory Museums and Gardens p. 56 (t); Picturepoint - London pp. 19 (tl), 35 (m), 42, 87, 90 (t); Royal Collection, reproduced by gracious permission of Her Majesty the Queen p. 52 (b); Royal Commission for Historical Monuments pp. 36, 46, 47 (l, r); St James' University Hospital, Leeds p. 61 (b); Scottish National Portrait Gallery p. 71; Will Wale p. 26 (m); Woodmansterne pp. 16 (t), 80 (b), 86 (t), 88 (b).

Causeway Press Ltd
PO Box 13, Ormskirk, Lancashire L39 5HP

© Ros Adams 1991

1st impression 1991

British Library Cataloguing in Publication Data
Adams, Ros
  Medieval Realms.
  I. Title
  942.02

  ISBN 0 946183 73 2

Typesetting by John A. Collins, Elaine Marie Cox (Picatype), Ormskirk, Lancashire L39 1QR (0695) 571197
Printed and bound by Butler & Tanner Ltd, Frome and London